MW00586352

TRUTH *with* LOVE

TRUTH *with* LOVE

The Apologetics of FRANCIS SCHAEFFER

BRYAN A. FOLLIS

CROSSWAY BOOKS

A PUBLISHING MINISTRY OF
GOOD NEWS PUBLISHERS
WHEATON, ILLINOIS

Truth with Love

Copyright © 2006 by Bryan A. Follis

Originally published by Titus Press, Belfast, Northern Ireland, 2005

First U.S. edition, 2006

Published by Crossway Books
    a publishing ministry of Good News Publishers
    1300 Crescent Street
    Wheaton, Illinois 60187

All rights reserved. No part of this publication may be reproduced, stored in a retrieval system or transmitted in any form by any means, electronic, mechanical, photocopy, recording or otherwise, without the prior permission of the publisher, except as provided by USA copyright law.

Cover design: Josh Dennis

First printing, 2006

Printed in the United States of America

Scripture quotations are taken from *The Holy Bible: English Standard Version*®. Copyright © 2001 by Crossway Bibles, a publishing ministry of Good News Publishers. Used by permission. All rights reserved.

Scripture quotations marked NIV are taken from *The Holy Bible: New International Version*®. Copyright © 1973, 1978, 1984 by International Bible Society. Used by permission of Zondervan Publishing House. All rights reserved. The "NIV" and "New International Version" trademarks are registered in the United States Patent and Trademark Office by International Bible Society. Use of either trademark requires the permission of International Bible Society.

Library of Congress Cataloging-in-Publication Data
Follis, Bryan A.
   Truth with love : the apologetics of Francis Schaeffer / Bryan A. Follis.
  —1st U.S. ed.
    p. cm.
   Originally published: Belfast, Northern Ireland : Titus Press, 2005.
   Includes bibliographical references.
  ISBN 13: 978-1-58134-774-6 (tpb)
  ISBN 10: 1-58134-774-X
   1. Schaeffer, Francis A. (Francis August) 2. Apologetics—History—
20th Century. I. Title
BT1117.F65   2006
230.092—dc22   2006015128

RRD		16	15	14	13	12	11	10	09	08	07	06
15	14	13	12	11	10	9	8	7	6	5	4	3	2	1

To
ELEANOR

We destroy arguments and every lofty opinion raised against the knowledge of God, and take every thought captive to obey Christ.

2 CORINTHIANS 10:5

Who is wise and understanding among you? By his good conduct let him show his works in the meekness of wisdom.

JAMES 3:13

CONTENTS

PREFACE

THIS BOOK DEVELOPED out of a dissertation I presented to Trinity College Dublin for the Senior Sophister. I was encouraged to expand it and seek publication. However, the reality of ordained ministry in a local church with its innumerable demands upon one's time has meant frequent delays in this writing project. Yet, I have also enjoyed some time off pastoral ministry, and so I wish to thank the officers of the congregation where I presently serve, All Saints' Church in Belfast, for kindly releasing me from duty during the final stages of the book.

Among those who have helped shape and sharpen my thinking, I am very grateful to those who agreed to be interviewed. In particular, I wish to thank Jerram Barrs, Andrew Fellows, Jim Ingram, Ranald Macaulay, Gavin McGrath, John and Prisci Sandri, Barry Seagren, and John Stott. Jock McGregor and William Barker kindly read earlier drafts and made very helpful comments. I am also indebted to William Edgar, who took time to read a draft of the entire manuscript and graciously pointed out some mistakes in my interpretation of Cornelius Van Til. I trust the final book has benefited from all these helpful contributions. However, where there are any remaining errors of fact, judgment, or interpretation, the blame lies totally with me.

This is my first book with Crossway, and I want to say what a delight it has been to work with them. My sincere thanks to Marvin Padgett, former Vice President of Editorial, who invited me to publish with Crossway; to Ted Griffin and Jill Carter who have gently (but very professionally) guided me through to production; and to those who

9

have worked so hard to design and market the book. I deeply appreciate the efforts of everyone at Crossway.

Above all, it is to my dear wife Eleanor that I owe the greatest thanks. Quite honestly, without her encouragement I doubt I would have found the motivation to resume writing; and without her willingness to sacrifice family time and accept a greater share of the household burdens, I know I would never have had the time to write. In recognition of this and given Eleanor's constant love, kindness, and support to me, it is a joy and a delight to dedicate this book to her.

Although I never met Francis Schaeffer, he has had a profound influence on me. It was through his film series *Whatever Happened to the Human Race?* that I was challenged and drawn back to Christ during a university mission. Thus I have retained a personal interest in his apologetics ever since. Then several years into my career (when I had a secular job), I realized that the reality of my faith in Christ was not as it once was. Reading Schaeffer on spirituality and then visiting L'Abri brought new and ongoing blessings. When Schaeffer is considered in the totality of his writings and ministry and we consider his stress on both rationality and spirituality, I believe he has still much to offer in the twenty-first century. It is with this conviction that I offer this book, in prayerful trust that the Lord may use it in some small way to help draw people closer unto Himself.

Bryan A. Follis

INTRODUCTION:
SCHAEFFER IN CONTEXT

THIS INTRODUCTION WILL outline the historical backdrop against which Francis Schaeffer lived and worked: the retreat of evangelicalism from its position in mainstream society to being a fringe separatist movement. In 1870 "almost all American Protestants thought of America as a Christian nation," and "Protestant evangelicals considered their faith to be the normative American creed."[1] However, intellectual challenges to this consensus "eventually made unbelief as respectable as belief among the country's intellectual elite."[2] As Nancy Pearcey has observed, Darwinism was "the missing puzzle piece that completed a naturalistic picture of reality."[3] Much of the advanced scholarship from Europe in philosophy, science, and biblical studies appeared to erode confidence in the truthfulness of Scripture.

There was soon a growing liberal or modernist approach among church scholars that sought to reinterpret the Christian faith in the light of such developments.[4] Modernism quickly won important victories in higher education, and by the early twentieth century it was exercising a growing influence within the Protestant churches. In reaction to this modernist trend, a series of pamphlets—*The Fundamentals: A Testimony to the Truth*—were published in 1910–1915 that restated the basic tenets of orthodox theology. These pamphlets (funded by evangelical businessmen from different denominations) gave name to the fundamentalist movement that was militantly anti-modernist.[5]

Although many of the original leaders of the movement were careful scholars such as Gresham Machen of Princeton, the momentum shifted toward what some writers have called "zealous but sometimes poorly informed persons."[6] The famous "Monkey Trial" in 1925 about the teaching of evolution in schools in Tennessee was a disaster for the image of Fundamentalism. The 1920s witnessed a series of defeats for the conservatives within the main Presbyterian church, and in 1929 Machen and three other faculty members withdrew from Princeton in protest at its proposed reorganization, which they believed was designed to destroy its distinctive anti-modernist character. Westminster Theological Seminary was established to promote an unmodified Calvinism and to continue the Old School theology of Princeton.[7]

The struggle against the modernists in relation to their control of the overseas missions board led to disciplinary action by the Presbyterian church against Machen and other conservative ministers who either resigned or were defrocked.[8] A new denomination—the Presbyterian Church of America (later renamed the Orthodox Presbyterian Church)—was launched to stand in "true spiritual succession" to the beliefs abandoned by the Presbyterian church.[9] Yet as a people they felt dispossessed. They had lost their original seminary and their original denomination, and they had passed from being leaders in a culturally powerful institution to being a very small, often ignored movement, and these experiences "tempted them at times to angry or bitter reactions."[10]

The failure of the attempt to combat modernism on an academic level weakened the conservative Presbyterian strand within the fundamentalist movement, and its predominant position was ended in 1937 with the death of Machen. Fundamentalism increasingly reflected the revivalist movement and the anti-intellectual populism of its grassroots evangelicalism.[11] In particular, premillennial dispensational theology became central to its self-understanding and the fundamentalist view of church and society.[12] A growing separatism from both liberal denominations and society characterized fundamentalists, and the intensity of the conflict pushed even less aggressive fundamentalists "toward sectarian and anti-intellectual affirmations of faith for fear of being labelled modernists."[13] In May 1937 the Orthodox Presbyterian Church (which Machen had founded) split, and a minority—who were premillennialists and strongly espoused total abstinence—founded the Bible Presbyterian Church. Oliver Buswell and Carl McIntire were among the leaders of the new denomination, which described itself as "Calvinistic, fundamental, premillennial and evangelistic."[14] The first minister to be ordained into the Bible Presbyterian Church was Francis Schaeffer.

FRANCIS SCHAEFFER

Born in 1912, Schaeffer grew up in a blue-collar family whose Christianity was only nominal. And the church he attended was very liberal. However, at the age of eighteen following a period of studying the Bible, he wrote in his diary on September 3, 1930, contrasting Scripture with secular philosophy, that "all truth is from the Bible" and converted from agnosticism to Christianity.[15] In 1935 he married Edith Seville, the daughter of former missionaries to China, and they subsequently had four children. Until his death in 1984, Edith was his soul mate, constant companion, and fellow soldier in the struggle to advance Christ's kingdom. Francis Schaeffer served three pastorates between 1938 and 1948 when he was sent to Europe by his denomination's board for international mission.[16] Based in Switzerland, Francis and Edith visited evangelical churches throughout western Europe—he to speak out against modernism and she to promote children's evangelism.

In 1951 Schaeffer faced a spiritual crisis, and among the various doubts and problems he had to wrestle with was the lack of love among many within the fundamentalist movement. Referring to the conflict with modernism, he wrote to a friend, "I think we have to be involved in the combat. But when we are fighting for the Lord, it has to be according to His rules, does it not?"[17] Gradually he saw the need to hold holiness in tension with love and to have a greater dependence upon the leading of the Holy Spirit. Returning to the United States on furlough in 1953, Schaeffer gave a series of sermons on the importance of true sanctification, but these addresses were badly received by many in leadership positions within the Bible Presbyterian Church. Yet Schaeffer was now convinced that

> if we are to know the fullest blessing of God, there must be no final loyalty to human leadership of organizations, or even to organizations as such. Rather, we must urge each other not even to give final authority to principles about Christ, but only to the person of Christ.[18]

Back in Switzerland, both Francis and Edith Schaeffer became increasingly convicted that the Lord was calling them into something new. Having experienced a number of difficulties and having received remarkable answers to prayer, the Schaeffers resigned from the mission board on June 4, 1955.[19] Having opened their home in Huémoz as L'Abri (which means "shelter"), they wanted to develop this and decided that they would "ask God that our work, and our lives, be a demonstration that He does exist."[20] The vision of L'Abri that was forming in Schaeffer's mind at this time was a place where he could help those in need, either spiritually or emotionally, whom God sent to him. The Schaeffers adopted as a guiding principle that "they would not publicise themselves but trust the Lord to send those people truly seeking and in need."[21] Looking back many years later on his spiritual crisis, Francis Schaeffer wrote:

> This was and is the real basis of L'Abri. Teaching the historic Christian answers and giving honest answers to honest questions are crucial; but it was out of these struggles that the reality came without which an incisive work like L'Abri would not have been possible.[22]

OUTLINE OF THE BOOK

This book aims to examine the apologetics of Francis Schaeffer and in particular to consider the role of reason and the importance of loving relationships. It also seeks to locate him within the Reformed tradition and to trace its varying intellectual influences on him. Chapter One will consider the importance of rationality in the writings of John Calvin and the different interpretations within the Reformed tradition (such as the Old Princetonians and Abraham Kuyper's Dutch School) of the use of reason in apologetics. Chapter Two will present a summary of Schaeffer's apologetical argument and explain how this must be understood in relation to his writings on spirituality and the way he actually conducted his discussions at L'Abri.

In Chapter Three we will analyze the role of reason in his apologetics and will consider criticism that Schaeffer drifted into rationalism. Chapter Four will explore the alternative view that Schaeffer's arguments were not rational enough and that his approach was that of a presuppositionalist. In rejecting this view, I will argue that Francis Schaeffer was more influenced by the verificationalist approach but that he should be seen primarily as an evangelist who pragmatically drew upon different streams. The Conclusion notes the development of postmodernism and questions whether the apologetics of Francis Schaeffer still has any relevance. I argue that the lack of trust today in the concept of truth makes his approach, with his strong emphasis on individual relationships, love, and truth, even more important.

1

CALVIN AND THE REFORMED
TRADITION

INTRODUCTION

To provide a benchmark against which to measure Francis Schaeffer, this chapter will examine John Calvin's views on the knowledge of God. In particular, as Calvin's writings often emerged in a polemic context, I wish to consider the point that his notion of the image of God in man took on different meanings in different contexts. This has led to different interpretations within the Reformed tradition of his teaching about the relationship of faith and reason. These different interpretations have thus affected the role accorded to reason in apologetics, and so distinctive schools of apologetics have developed.[1] This chapter will therefore also explain the different approaches of some key Reformed thinkers who have exercised an influence on Francis Schaeffer. This will help us evaluate Schaeffer's own style of apologetics.

CALVIN AND PHILOSOPHY IN CONTEXT

Given the fact that within Reformed Christianity the Scriptures occupy a primary place in Christian epistemology, some Reformed writers stress that without God's revelation "we cannot trust reason, sense experience, intuition, or any other methods purporting to give knowledge."[2] Sometimes in their eagerness to distinguish Calvin's approach from that of the Roman Catholic philosopher and theologian Thomas Aquinas (1225–1274), it is stated that Calvin found knowledge of God in Scripture alone. However, Calvin's teachings on the sources of our knowledge of God are more complex than some are willing to accept. Calvin needs to be understood in the context of his time, and that means recognizing the intellectual influences that guided his thinking.

Calvin, more than Luther, came from a background colored by Renaissance humanism, and there was some continuity of thought with the humanist tradition after his conversion.[3] Rejecting the other-worldliness of medieval scholasticism (which had developed from the writings of Thomas Aquinas), this humanism accepted the worth of earthly existence for its own sake. Following the French humanists, Calvin decried what he perceived as an overreliance on reason by the scholastics. He also attacked the scholastics for their view that grace is both operative (given by God alone) and cooperative (man working with God). Calvin believed that this implied a natural ability in human nature to seek the good. Indeed for the Reformers, the abuses of the medieval church and its whole penitential system resulted from a false epistemology. It was wrong knowledge that led to wrong practice, for a "natural knowledge of God is void of true soteriological [i.e., saving] knowledge."[4] Some Reformed commentators trace this to Aquinas, whom they view as the first great proponent of a natural theology distinguishable from revealed theology. He sought to draw upon the philosophy of Aristotle (384–322 B.C.) and to reclaim reason as a tool in Christian theology. Andrew Hoffecker has even suggested that the synthesis produced by Aquinas included heretical elements from Pelagius (a fourth-century monk) insofar as reason remains "unscathed by the fall, and the will is only partially debilitated by sin."[5]

Although Calvin criticized those who followed Aristotle for their reliance on human reason and free will, and Zwingli, who led the Reformation in Zurich, was outspoken in his anti-scholasticism and anti-Aristotelianism, it is wrong to view the Reformation as completely overthrowing the Aristotelian inheritance bequeathed by Aquinas. Indeed as Alister McGrath has noted, Aristotelianism stubbornly persisted in Renaissance humanism to "the intense irritation of those who prefer to regard the Renaissance as essentially a Platonist reaction against scholastic Aristotelianism."[6] Calvin was interested in humanism's concept of natural law, and it is inconceivable that there was no Aristotelian influence in this. Colin Brown finds not only similarities between Calvin and Aquinas but also extensive use of Aristotelian ideas by Calvin, not least in his articulation of the doctrine of election and predestination. Brown regards it as "tantalizing" to ask about philosophical influences on Calvin, and he speculates as to whether the Reformer's doctrines were "purely and simply biblical theology" as he believed them to be.[7] However, without further evidence this is only speculation. Furthermore, recognizing a residual Aristotelianism in Calvin's thought—such as Aristotle's concept of a fourfold causality—does not allow us to say that his theology was not under the supremacy of Scripture. Indeed, in a comparison of Calvin's exposition of Romans 9 (on election and predestination) with that by Aquinas, Steinmetz found that several of Aquinas's most characteristic modifications of the Augustinian tradition found "no corresponding echo" in Calvin's exposition.[8]

While Calvin was prepared to draw upon non-scriptural sources, they were always subservient to Scripture and often used to confirm it, as is seen in his dialogue with Cicero in the *Institutes of the Christian Religion*. As McGrath notes, Calvin accepted classical wisdom in Christian theology "in that it demonstrates the necessity of, and partially verifies the substance of, divine revelation."[9] But when any secular or religious teaching or philosophical ideas were contrary to Scripture, such as natural theology on the scholastic pattern, Calvin regarded them as inadmissible. This was the same approach as that to his use of Patristic sources (which he frequently quoted). Calvin treats "the Fathers as partners in conversation rather than as authorities in the medieval sense of the term. They stimulate Calvin in his reflections on the text. . . . Nevertheless, they do not have the last word. Paul does."[10] Yet Calvin did not say that without Scripture man does not have some natural consciousness of God. He believed that "there exists in the human mind, and indeed by natural instinct, some sense of Deity."[11] What we need to consider is just what Calvin meant by this.

THE IMAGE OF GOD

The Bible states that to be human means to be made "in the image of God," but the relevant passages (Genesis 1:26-27; 5:1-2; 9:6-7) do not define precisely what this means. For Augustine—from whose intellectual well Calvin was to drink deeply—it was the human capacity to reason that distinguished human from animal nature and by which contact was made with the divine. Although Augustine saw knowing God as primarily an intellectual matter, Sherlock argues, it was not a rationalistic understanding of "image" in that something far richer than mere "head knowledge" (i.e., creative thought) was meant.[12] Modern writers tend to have a very restrictive view of reason, and it is important that we do not read back into Augustine a contemporary understanding that is less than his concept of creative thought. Returning to the issue of the image of God in mankind, was it completely lost in the Fall? If one stresses the relational character of the image—that one stands in proper relationship with God—then for Calvin the image was destroyed by the Fall. However, Calvin also maintained that man still enjoyed "noble endowments which bespeak the divine presence with us."[13]

Brian Gerrish has noted that "scholars have found an ambiguity in Calvin's answer to the question: 'Is the image of God lost in the fallen man?'"[14] However, this apparent contradiction in Calvin's thought is resolved when we understand the comprehensive conception he had of the image of God. Luther did not "seek the image of God in any of the natural endowments of man, such as his rational and moral powers, but exclusively in original righteousness, and therefore regarded it as entirely lost by sin."[15] By contrast, Calvin believed that the image of God extends to everything that makes human nature distinct from the other species of animals, and while the whole image was damaged by sin, only the spiritual qualities were completely lost. Indeed he said, "since reason, by which man discerns between good and evil, and by which he understands and judges, is a natural gift, it could not be entirely destroyed."[16] Man did not become a brute animal; he is still man, for in spite of his fall "there are still some sparks which show that he is a rational animal." Calvin was convinced "that one of the essential properties of our nature is reason, which distinguishes us from the lower animals."[17] Yet Calvin did not regard man as being made in the image of God simply because he has reason. Rather, as Edward Dowey points out, the ability to reflect God's glory and worship Him was also a key distinguishing characteristic.[18]

Although humanity retains the image of God (albeit in a reduced form), Calvin argued that this light was "so smothered by clouds of darkness" that in relation to a saving knowledge of God, people were "blinder than moles."[19] Nevertheless, Calvin is keen to stress Paul's teaching that though we are unable without divine revelation to rise to a pure and clear knowledge of God, we cannot plead ignorance. Drawing upon Romans 1:18-28, Calvin argued that verse 20 clearly teaches that since people may know about God from His created world, they are "without excuse" and hence have "an utter incapacity to bring any defence to prevent them from being justly accused before the judgement-seat of God."[20] However, this knowledge about God is not saving knowledge of God and is inadequate because of our blindness. We are not so blind that we don't realize the necessity of worshiping God, but our judgment "fails here before it discovers the nature or character of God." The problem is not a lack of evidence or knowledge but a moral deficiency: we refuse to submit to the evidence that God provides. For Calvin (as for Paul) we see enough to keep us from making excuses, but our blindness prevents us from reaching our goal, and it is only by the gift of faith and its light that "man can gain real knowledge from the work of creation."[21]

THE CHARACTER OF OUR KNOWLEDGE

Medieval scholasticism taught that there is a natural law—i.e., a moral order divinely implanted in all people that is accessible by reason.[22] At times Calvin seems to go along with this view, but at other times he appears to stress that without divine revelation man would be left in a state of agnosticism. However, not in vain has God

> added the light of his Word in order that he might make himself known unto salvation, and bestowed the privilege on those whom he was pleased to bring into nearer and more familiar relation to himself.[23]

Susan Schreiner suggests that Calvin's notion of the image of God took on different meanings in different contexts, though not, she argues, contradictory meanings.[24] It is important to bear this in mind as we consider Calvin's understanding of the character of our knowledge of God.

Calvin speaks of a double knowledge: the "simple and primitive knowledge to which the mere course of nature would have conducted us, had Adam stood upright" and the saving knowledge revealed through Scripture that focuses upon the life, death, and resurrection of Jesus Christ who paid the penalty due to us, by which "salvation was obtained for us by his righteousness."[25] Creation continues to provide to all people important points of contact with God, but in His mercy to His Church, God supplements "these common proofs by the addition of his Word, as a surer and more direct means of discovering himself."[26]

Calvin believed that Scripture only gives "a saving knowledge of God when its certainty is founded on the inward persuasion of the Holy Spirit."[27] Thus it is foolish to attempt to prove to nonbelievers that Scripture is the Word of God as it can only be known as such by faith. Taken in isolation—as it sometimes is—this appears to commit Calvin to fideism—i.e., the view that our knowledge of God is solely based on faith apart from any evidence or rational considerations. However, Calvin accepted that there were also rational grounds for arguing that Scripture is the Word of God and such human testimonies "which go to confirm it will not be without effect, if they are used in subordination to that chief and highest proof [the Holy Spirit], as secondary helps to our weakness." He devoted a chapter in the *Institutes* to proving the credibility of Scripture "in so far as natural reason admits."

While recognizing that such proofs were only "secondary helps," Calvin seeks to argue against those who ask how we can know that Moses and the prophets wrote the books that bear their names and even "dare to question whether there ever was a Moses." He draws upon both internal literary evidence and historical background to confirm belief in the Scriptures as God's Word, while he regards the "many striking miracles" and fulfillment of divine prophecy as validating Moses and the prophets as messengers of God's Word.[28] Calvin finds the very survival of the Scriptures over the centuries to be proof of their divine origin, given the intensity of human opposition to them. He believed that the highest proof of Scripture is taken from the character of Him whose Word it is. If people were reasonable and looked at Scripture "with clear eyes and unbiased judgment, it will forthwith present itself with a divine majesty which will subdue our presumptuous opposition, and force us to do it homage." Nevertheless, Calvin knew that even if you establish the Scriptures as the Word of God in discussion with non-believers, it does "not follow that we shall forthwith implant the certainty which faith requires in their hearts."[29] The Holy Spirit must seal the truth in people's minds.

Yet Calvin's willingness to use rational argument about God in preliminary discussion with nonbelievers and to strengthen the faith of believers shows him to be no fideist. He is balanced in his teaching about the positive role of reason in what we would now call apologetics, while still maintaining that the testimony of the Spirit is superior to reason. This balanced approach is also seen in his teaching about the Word and the Spirit working together and his warning against "giddy men" who make "a great display of the superiority of the Spirit and reject all reading of the Scriptures."[30] Calvin's writings on human nature and the knowledge of God were, as Schreiner points out, "often developed polemically and require attention both to this polemical context and to the perspective out of which he spoke."[31] This explains why Calvin's notion of the image of God took on different meanings in different contexts.

CALVIN AND NATURAL LAW

John McNeill has suggested that there was no disagreement between the Scholastic tradition and the Reformers on the subject of natural law, and that might explain why his discussions of it (according to Schreiner) seem "imprecise and unsystematic."[32] Calvin assumed that Scripture, particularly Romans 2:14-15, affirmed the existence of natural law, and in his commentary on this passage he stated that it is beyond all doubt that all men "have certain ideas of justice and rectitude which are implanted by nature in the hearts of men."[33] Apart from the scriptural basis for natural law, Calvin also argued from experience that in addition to naturally knowing right from wrong, people realize in their hearts (as we have already said) that there is a God and that honor and worship are due to Him. Writing in his *Institutes*, he stated that the human conscience challenges those who would do wrong, and "every man, being stung by the consciousness of his own unhappiness, in this way necessarily obtains at least some knowledge of God." Furthermore, the experience of observing the world around us and the glory of God that is engraved on it means that "we cannot open our eyes without being compelled to behold him."[34]

Brown thinks that some might find it strange that Calvin was content to use non-scriptural arguments in this way, but he maintains that if all people "really have a sense of deity, scriptural proof is not needed. If they have got it, they have got it."[35] Calvin had no objection to using argument from outside Scripture for the necessity of revelation. He was ready to employ argument from either experience or natural law to make his point. For example, when opposing those who followed Plato and Aristotle and their reliance on human reason and free will, Calvin used natural law to disprove "the Platonic theory that sin resulted from ignorance."[36] This perhaps reflects his eclectic use of philosophy, which Dowey believes indicates that Calvin was not really "interested in technical epistemology."[37] Calvin was also content to draw upon tradition in the form of Augustine and Bernard of Clairvaux to argue that the Fall did not eradicate the activity of the will but that the will (albeit enslaved) is never passive, and even when people can only will in the direction of evil, they choose to do so, for people act "voluntarily and not by compulsion."[38]

As Schreiner says, Calvin was not so much interested in natural law in itself but as an idea to explain the continuation of society after the devastating effects of the Fall. The survival and stability of society were due not only to the restraining aspects of divine providence but also to the spiritual remnant of the divine image within each person. Calvin argued that man "is disposed, from natural instinct, to cherish and preserve society," and "some principle of civil order is impressed on all."[39] Calvin also accepted the distinction between the two realms of existence (i.e., heavenly and earthly) to show how (within the earthly realm) our natural abilities and insights in medicine, science, the arts, and manual skills are blessings to be used "for the common benefit of mankind."[40] Believing that society was the arena in which Christians should seek their holiness, Calvin believed that all have a divine calling to fulfill the cultural mandate, but in doing so we "must exercise moderation, patience, and fidelity in our daily vocation, working as unto the Lord before the face of God."[41]

Faith and Reason: Different Reformed Interpretations

In turning from Calvin himself to the role of reason in the Reformed tradition, we notice a variety of interpretations. While this section will examine some of the different interpretations, it is not intended to be a comprehensive history of Reformed thought on the subject. Instead it will highlight a few key Reformed thinkers who have influenced Schaeffer so that we may understand him in context. The different interpretations of the role of reason arise from multiple readings of Calvin's writings. As noted above, Calvin was not developing a theology of natural law, and perhaps that is why McGrath suggests that his writings on natural law were "sufficiently ambiguous to permit any number of theories and applications."[42] Although Protestantism is less closely associated with natural law than is Roman Catholicism, it is Calvinism that has provided the stage for debate over the past century about natural law and in particular about common grace. Abraham Kuyper, founder of the Free University of Amsterdam, is best remembered for his development of the theological doctrine of common grace. In this he argued that common grace is the foundation of civilized society, since God's great plan for Creation is achieved through common grace. Common grace is so called because it is believed to be common to all people. Among its benefits is a consciousness within every person "of the difference between right and wrong, truth and falsehood, justice and injustice."[43]

Without wishing to deny the doctrine of total depravity, Kuyper gave to common grace an independent role that helped make history and culture possible. Thus he argued that the "tendency in devout circles to oppose the progress and perpetual development of human life was therefore quite misguided."[44] Indeed he urged that the "view that would confine God's work to the small sector we might label 'church life' must be set side . . . for common grace encompasses the whole life of the world."[45] While there has been considerable controversy over the doctrine of common grace, there has never been complete agreement within the Reformed churches about Calvin's teaching on the image of God. Berkhof points out that some have held to a restricted view (i.e., that the image of God be understood in terms of our relationship to Him and thus to have been destroyed by the Fall). However, it was the broader conception of the image of God (i.e., that the image also includes that which makes human nature distinct) "which became the prevalent one in Reformed theology."[46]

Jonathan Edwards (1703–1758), who has been described by Robert Jenson as the "greatest American Divine," is an example of a Reformed thinker who gave a broader interpretation to the image of God. He regarded man's natural reason as "the highest faculty we have," and he believed that even the heathen realized that "the main business of man was the improvement and exercise of his understanding."[47] Yet, as Edwards argued, the purpose for which God had given mankind the faculty of understanding was that "he might understand divine things."[48] However, in view of man's fallen state, divinity could not be learned "merely by the improvement of man's natural reason"[49] but required God's revelation in Scripture. Nevertheless, Edwards still envisaged a key role for reason as man came to know about God. He distinguished between a "natural" and "spiritual" type of divine knowledge, with the former being obtainable by the "natural exercise of our faculties."[50] He therefore encouraged Christians to seek "by reading and other proper means, a good rational knowledge of the things of divinity."[51]

Yet Edwards realized that "there is a difference between having a right speculative notion of the doctrines contained in the word of God, and having a due sense of them in the heart."[52] As James Packer has observed, for Edwards salvation was more "than an intellectual grasp of theological ideas . . . [it was] rather, the result of direct divine illumination accompanying the written or spoken word of God."[53] This may appear to contradict the earlier statement that reason plays a key role in a person's coming to know God. However, any apparent contradiction is resolved by grasping Edwards's understanding of the actual role of reason. While recognizing the limitation of any knowledge of God obtained by reasoning alone, he argued that we cannot enjoy a "spiritual" knowledge without first having a "natural" (or rational) knowledge of divine things. Thus the "special illumination of the Spirit of God" was not some abstract or mystical experience, for he was convinced that "God deals with man as with a rational creature."[54] Hence "no object can come at the heart but through the door of the understanding: and there can be no spiritual knowledge of that of which there is not first a rational knowledge."[55] Reason, for Edwards, was inadequate but essential: before one can know God, one has to know *about* God.

In nineteenth-century America, Princeton became the premier seminary of Reformed scholarship, and B. B. Warfield, who taught there from 1887 until 1921, was its preeminent professor of theology. Dr. Carl Trueman suggests that "we have no one like him today in terms of the sweep of his interests and his apparently omnivorous theological mind."[56] Warfield frequently asserted that the Christian faith is a reasonable faith based on good and sufficient evidence, not a blind and ungrounded faith.[57] Apologetics was therefore highly rated, and he even argued that "it is impossible to form any vital conception of God without some movement of intellect."[58] Warfield also argued that Calvin saw a role for theistic proofs (i.e., arguments proving the existence of God), albeit with value more "for developing the knowledge of God than merely establishing His existence."[59] Warfield felt that theistic proofs were "objectively valid" but recognized that they could not "work true faith apart from the testimony of the Spirit."[60] In other words, one cannot argue someone into the kingdom of God purely through intellectual persuasion. Nevertheless, he maintained that rational argument or apologetics plays a vital role since faith is "a form of conviction and is therefore, necessarily grounded in evidence. . . . Christianity makes its appeal to right reason."[61]

THE ROLE OF REASON

This emphasis on the role of reason has led some scholars, Peter Hicks being one, to conclude that Warfield "put more confidence in rational argument" than Reformed scholars in previous generations.[62] Indeed Alister McGrath even claims to trace a "strongly rationalistic tone" in the writings of Warfield and notes with concern that Princeton absorbed uncritically a number of foundational Enlightenment assumptions. This led, he argues, to "a questionably high estimation of the role of reason in theology."[63] Warfield, along with Princeton in general, conducted theology in an epistemological structure provided by Scottish Common Sense philosophy. This philosophy held that "reality of the self, the law of non-contradiction, reliability of sense perception, and basic cause-and-effect connections provide people with considerable knowledge about nature and human nature."[64] Although Calhoun argues that the "Princetonians never allowed Scottish Common Sense philosophy to stand by itself or to determine their theological outlook,"[65] it is clear that as an epistemological system it allowed the development of one's theology in any particular direction. For example, building upon the same philosophical foundations, Yale developed a liberal theology, while Harvard was Unitarian in its outlook. Vander Molen suggests that there was a "rather easy accommodation of philosophy and theology" in Scottish Common Sense philosophy, and by being so amenable to the use of reason it enabled Reformed scholars to "adapt to modern rationalist and Enlightenment philosophy quite easily."[66]

Abraham Kuyper, coming out of a Dutch tradition that sharply criticized Enlightenment thought, was ready to offer a critique of the Princeton approach.[67] For Kuyper, the consequence of the Fall was a radically abnormal world, and he held that only "the sovereign, regenerating work of the Holy Spirit can overcome the rebellion of unbelief. An absolute antithesis exists in all of life (including all scholarly work) between believer and unbeliever."[68] Whereas for apologists influenced by Common Sense, sin "was a factor which could prevent one taking an objective look at the evidence for the truth of divine things, for Kuyper unacknowledged sinfulness inevitably blinded one from true knowledge of God."[69] Kuyper maintained that no one could achieve a knowledge of God through rational argument, "where reason is both a party to the dispute and its judge."[70] Thus he believed that only as God Himself breathes into the fallen minds of humans could He be known, and Kuyper argued that this work of the Holy Spirit provided "its own certainty."[71] Hence while Warfield held that it was the task of apologetics to lay the foundations for theology, Kuyper took the opposite view and regarded theology as the starting point for apologetics.

Through Dutch emigration to America and the subsequent founding of their own denomination and college (i.e., the Christian Reformed Church and Calvin College), coupled with Kuyper's visit to America in 1898, his writings began to be more widely known.[72] In the twentieth century a school of Reformed apologetics developed among those influenced by Kuyper that views as futile, and even unfaithful, the attempts of traditional apologetics to prove the existence of God by argument. Recognizing that all views of reality begin with certain ideas or presuppositions that exercise an enormous, though often unacknowledged, influence over what and how we know, it is argued that one must presuppose God before one can prove anything.[73] Under Cornelius Van Til, who taught apologetics at Westminster Theological Seminary from 1929 until 1972, this presuppositional apologetics has become the majority view within contemporary Reformed apologetics. Although Van Til argued that all intelligibility depends on or presupposes Christian theism, he was willing to "place himself upon the position of his opponent" merely "for argument's sake" in order to show him or her that on such a position the "facts" that he or she looks to are not facts.[74] As William Edgar has pointed out, Schaeffer's favorite method in apologetics (pushing an unbeliever to the extreme of his or her own presuppositions to show how dark the world is without Christ) was "very similar, if not identical" to Van Til's idea of placing yourself on your opponent's ground for the sake of argument.[75]

Conclusion

Because of such similarities, some, including Forrest Baird, believe that Francis Schaeffer was "heavily influenced by Van Til."[76] But it is important to note that Gresham Machen—whom we discussed in the Introduction—also had a profound effect on Schaeffer's thinking. Machen sought to continue the Old Princetonian approach of rational apologetical argument, and he was convinced that should God send a revival, one of the means that the Holy Spirit would use "is an awakening of the intellect."[77] Schaeffer, as we shall examine in Chapter Four, drew upon the Old Princetonian approach and the presuppositionalism of Van Til to develop a new style of apologetics. Because of this blending of different apologetical models mixed with some originality on his own part, many scholars have difficulty in reaching agreement about Schaeffer's methodology.[78] However, Schaeffer made no definitive claims for his style of apologetics, and although he believed that unless "our epistemology is right everything is going to be wrong,"[79] he did not even regard himself as an academic apologist.[80] His principal interest was evangelism, and apologetics was but a means to that end, for Francis Schaeffer was convinced that if the Christian faith is to be effectively communicated, "we must know and understand the thought-forms of our own generation."[81]

This chapter has sought to demonstrate the complexity of Calvin's understanding of the image of God. Although he maintained that the relational aspects of the image had been destroyed by the Fall, he believed that people still retained a divine presence in that, among other things, they were rational creatures. A certain ambiguity in Calvin's writings has led some Reformed thinkers to give particular emphases to different aspects of his teaching. As shown, this has resulted in the emergence of distinctive schools of Reformed apologetics, each according a different status to the role of reason. By placing him in context and explaining his intellectual roots, this chapter has set the scene for Francis Schaeffer. We will now consider his own approach to apologetics, in terms both of the rational arguments he used and of the importance he gave to love as the "final apologetic."

2

ARGUMENTS AND
APPROACH

INTRODUCTION

This chapter will present a broad outline of Schaeffer's apologetics and will consider how he sought to communicate the gospel in terms the present generation could understand. In view of the distinctive person-centered approach taken at L'Abri, we will give attention not only to *what* Schaeffer said, but also to the *why* and the *how* of the way he conducted apologetics.

Francis Schaeffer wrote twenty-three books that have been translated into twenty-five languages and have sold three million copies. Not surprisingly, he was described as "among the most influential conservative evangelical leaders in recent decades."[1] He has been praised for helping make evangelicalism intellectually respectable through his analysis of contemporary problems, his evaluation of possible philosophical and theological solutions, and his presentation of a coherent Christianity. However, as James Packer has pointed out, it is wrong to think that Schaeffer was "trying to be a pioneer theoretician in philosophy and apologetics."[2] Indeed Schaeffer did not regard himself as creating an apologetic system and stated that he did not believe "there is any one apologetic which meets the needs of all people."[3]

He saw himself as an evangelist who dealt with philosophical, intellectual, and cultural questions as part of his work in leading people to Jesus Christ. Harold Brown is right to suggest that even when dealing with the big issues that were his speciality, Schaeffer treated them not as theoretical problems to be fitted into a comprehensive world view, but as questions that individual persons needed to answer in order to find meaning in their lives.[4]

Schaeffer had very little time for an academic apologetic that just seemed to argue a philosophical point for the sake of it. He directly linked apologetics with evangelism and felt that it was not really Christian apologetics if it did not "lead people to Christ as Saviour and then on to their living under the Lordship of Christ in the whole of life."[5]

Understanding the Truth

Packer is correct in believing that Schaeffer perceived the primacy of thought in each individual's makeup, so that "how we think determines what we are."[6] Schaeffer was convinced that because Christianity is a specific body of truth, "knowledge is needed prior to salvation."[7] Thus he maintained that "it must be the whole man who comes to understand that the gospel is truth and believes because he is convinced on the basis of good and sufficient reason that it is truth."[8]

This does not, however, mean that everyone is to be treated as an intellectual nor that a person lacking in intellectual ability, as understood in an academic sense, is unable to understand the truth of the gospel. We should never confuse rationality with intellectualism, nor should we forget, as C. S. Lewis reminds us, that "uneducated people are not irrational people."[9] All people are made in the image of God, and rationality, as Chapter One demonstrated, is an expression of that. As human beings we are made for truth because we are made in God's image. Schaeffer knew from his own life that it is not just academics who ask questions about Christianity and who need to be persuaded about its truth-claims. He noted that he had

worked with shipyard workers, mill workers, all kinds of people (as well as, when I was younger, personally working on farms, a huckster wagon, in factories, and so on), and I am convinced that these people often have the same questions as the intellectual; the only thing is that they do not articulate them, or if they do articulate them it is not in the same terminology.[10]

Given that God made the whole person and is interested in the whole person, his or her mind included, Schaeffer believed that true salvation is "a salvation which touches the whole man."[11] For Schaeffer, as already stated, that involved a person's coming to believe the gospel on the basis of good and sufficient reason. Yet he recognized that in attempting to communicate the truth of the gospel, the Church was facing a rapidly changing historical situation. Thus if you wanted people to understand what you were saying, you needed to know their thought-forms and communicate accordingly. Schaeffer argued that unless Christians did this, "the unchangeable principles of Christianity will fall on deaf ears."[12] The change in thought-forms, and in particular the change in the concept of truth, made communication of the gospel to the younger generation extremely difficult. Indeed Schaeffer was convinced that this was the "most crucial problem" facing Christianity because before a man "is ready to become a Christian, he must have a proper understanding of truth."[13]

The three books he was invited to publish in 1968, 1969, and 1972—*The God Who Is There*, *Escape from Reason*, and *He Is There and He Is Not Silent*—reveal Schaeffer to be someone with clear insight into the modern secular world and its thought-forms. Schaeffer felt that these three books "constitute a conscious unity" and contribute to the task of "speaking historic Christianity into the twentieth century."[14] Certainly they established him and his apologetics within evangelical Christianity. For example, *The God Who Is There* sold over four hundred thousand copies. Because Schaeffer is best known through these three books, and they are seen as comprising the core of his apologetical writing, I shall mainly concentrate on them in this section. However, as will later be argued, we need to move beyond these three books if we want to fully understand Schaeffer's apologetics.

Truth as an Absolute

In *The God Who Is There* Schaeffer tackled the problem of how to communicate Christian truth to people who no longer believe in truth as an absolute or as an antithesis. Traditionally, people had believed in absolutes, and since absolutes imply antithesis, "they took it for granted that if anything was true, the opposite was false."[15] This meant that even if a person did not accept the truth of the gospel, he or she understood what you were talking about. Thus the change in the concept of truth away from absolutes and antithesis created major problems for the evangelist, given "that historic Christianity stands on a basis of antithesis. Without it, historic Christianity is meaningless."[16] Schaeffer believed that people in Europe prior to about 1890 and in America prior to about 1935 lived by presuppositions that in practice seemed to accord with the Christian's own presuppositions. By *presupposition* he meant a belief held by a person that "often consciously or unconsciously affects the way a person subsequently reasons."[17] Although people may have disagreed as to what their absolutes were, nevertheless they agreed that there were absolutes, and so "they could reason together on the classical basis of antithesis."[18] With the shift to synthesis (i.e., the combination of the partial truths of a thesis and its antithesis), classical apologetics is no longer feasible because it fails to "understand the importance of combating a false set of presuppositions."[19]

To explain how the shift in secular society took place, Schaeffer presented a historical sweep from Thomas Aquinas (1225–1274) to the present day that sought to cover the key disciplines of philosophy, theology, and art. He traced the origins of the modern outlook to the teaching of Aquinas and his view of grace and nature. He believed that Aquinas had an incomplete view of the Fall, whereby while the will of man was fallen, the intellect was not. From this, as time passed, man's intellect was seen as autonomous, and one result was the development of natural theology, a theology that could be pursued independently of the Scriptures. In *Escape from Reason* Schaeffer argued that this opened up an area of thought that became autonomous from God, and on the basis of this autonomous principle, "philosophy also became increasingly free, and was separated from revelation."[20] Indeed, the autonomous principle did not remain confined to philosophy or theology but soon entered art and began to influence general culture. Schaeffer believed that once nature (i.e., the created order) is made autonomous, it begins to "eat up" grace (i.e., God the Creator), and for him this reached a climax at the high point of the Renaissance. While he welcomed the correction from overemphasis on heavenly things that Renaissance thought provided, Schaeffer noted that there was much that was destructive—nature ate up grace until grace was dead.[21]

Particulars Without Meaning

For Schaeffer another unfortunate consequence of Aquinas's teaching was a dichotomy between universals and particulars. In nature you have particulars (i.e., individual things), while in grace you have the universal (i.e., that which covers all the particulars and gives them meaning).[22] Schaeffer believed that Aristotle, whose philosophy influenced Aquinas, emphasized the particulars rather than the universal that gave unity to all the particulars. However, once you set the particulars free, how do you hold them together?[23] Where do you find unity? Where do you find meaning? Schaeffer maintained that this marks the drift toward modern man and his cynicism.

> [W]e are left with masses of particulars but no way to get them together. So we find that by this time nature is eating up grace in the area of morals, and even more basically, in the area of epistemology as well.[24]

Yet despite the lower elements eating up the higher elements, what Schaeffer calls the "lower story" and the "upper story," man did not "abandon the hope of a rational unity between the particulars and the universal."[25] For this reason Schaeffer regarded Leonardo da Vinci as an important figure. He understood that if you emphasize the particulars and begin

> on the basis of rationalism—that is, man beginning only from himself, and not having any outside knowledge—you would only . . . end up with mechanics . . . there were not going to be any universals or meaning at all.[26]

Leonardo realized that this would not do and tried to produce the universal by painting the soul. He failed but "never gave up the hope of a unified field of knowledge."[27]

Schaeffer identifies a paradigm shift by the time of Jean-Jacques Rousseau (1712–1778)—from nature and grace to nature and freedom. Nature had totally devoured grace, and there was no concept of revelation in any area. What was left in its place in the upper story was freedom. Partly as a reaction to the determinism that began to emerge from nature's being so autonomous, thinkers like Rousseau longed for freedom. It is a freedom that is in itself as autonomous as nature, and so "it means a freedom in which the individual is the centre of the universe." Schaeffer believed that it is a freedom with nothing to restrain it, and "it is a freedom that no longer fits into the rational world."[28] Meanwhile, as scientists shifted their presuppositions to embrace a worldview that understands reality only in materialist and naturalist terms, they came to believe in "the uniformity of natural causes in a closed system."[29] Indeed their naturalism was so closed and their system so determinist, Schaeffer suggests, that they treated everything as if it were a machine. However, given that they still insisted on a unity of knowledge, it was a unity achieved simply by ruling out freedom. The "upper story" completely disappears: neither "God nor freedom are there anymore—everything is in the machine."[30]

THE LINE OF DESPAIR

The search of rationalism for an answer that would encompass all of thought and all of life did not prove successful. Throughout the Enlightenment people continued to think that they could construct a unified field of knowledge "by means of rationalism plus rationality."[31] By "rationalism" Schaeffer meant man beginning absolutely and totally from himself, gathering information concerning the particulars, and formulating the universal. For Schaeffer "rationality" means mankind thinking in a way that is not contrary to reason, or as he put it, "man's aspiration of reason is valid." He maintained that rationality always involves antithesis, for "that is the way God has made us, and there is no other way to think."[32] By the time of Immanuel Kant (1774–1804), the philosophers

came to the realization that they could not find this unified rationalistic circle and so, departing from the classical methodology of antithesis, they shifted the concept of truth, and modern man was born.[33]

Schaeffer believed that this set the stage for Friedrich Hegel (1770–1831), who opened the door to "the line of despair." This was a "titanic shift," for previously people above the line had been "rationalistic optimists" who sought an adequate explanation for the whole of reality "without having to depart from the logic of antithesis."[34] Now absolute truth was displaced, and "all possible positions are relativized and truth is to be sought in synthesis rather than antithesis."[35] Schaeffer argues that this move—whereby mankind retained his rationalism but at the expense of rationality—was made out of desperation, but that this is characteristic of sinful man. Placing himself, rather than God, at the center of the universe and making himself autonomous, man will give up his rationality so he can preserve his rationalism, his autonomy, and his rebellion against God.[36] Schaeffer maintained that following Hegel, "truth as truth was gone, and synthesis (the both-and), with its relativism, reigns." Schaeffer declared that a

> central reason Christians do not understand their children is because their children no longer think in the same framework in which their parents think. It is not merely that they come out with different answers. The methodology has changed—that is, the very method by which they arrive at, or try to arrive at, truth has changed.[37]

THE LEAP OF FAITH

Although Hegel opened "the line of despair" (i.e., abandoning all hope of finding a unified answer for knowledge and life), Schaeffer held that it was Søren Kierkegaard (1813–1855) who was the first thinker to go below it. Hegel can be classified as an idealist, and certainly "he thought that in practice synthesis could be arrived at by reason." However, this did not prove possible, and Kierkegaard concluded that you "achieve everything of real importance by a leap of faith."[38] With Kierkegaard, the line between nature and universals widened considerably, and indeed there was now no interchange. Below the line there is rationality and logic, while the upper story becomes the non-rational and non-logical. As Schaeffer noted, in the lower story, on the basis of reason, "man has no meaning, no purpose, no significance. There is only pessimism concerning man as man. But up above, on the basis of a nonrational, nonreasonable leap, there is a nonreasonable faith which gives optimism."[39] Thus, given the total separation of faith from the rational, if

> rationalistic man wants to deal with the really important things of human life (such as purpose, significance, the validity of love), he must discard rational thought about them and make a gigantic, nonrational leap of faith.[40]

Schaeffer regarded Kierkegaard as the father of modern existential thinking in both its secular and theological forms. Given that existentialism was extremely fashionable in the 1960s when Schaeffer was speaking and writing, he looked at Jean-Paul Sartre (1905–1980) and Karl Jaspers (1883–1969). Rationally, Sartre found the universe absurd, and so he encouraged people to "authenticate" themselves by an act of the will. Yet as Schaeffer explained, "authentication has no rational or logical content—all directions of the will are equal."[41] Jaspers spoke of a "final experience" that would be so big in your life that it would give you a certainty that you are there and that you have a hope of meaning. However, given that the "final experience" is "totally separated from the rational, there is no way to communicate its content either to someone else or to yourself."[42] Having helped a student who was close to suicide as he attempted to cling to the fading memory of his final experience, Schaeffer lamented, "how hopeless is hope based only on this final experience."[43] Yet because mankind is made in the image of God, he cannot live as though he is nothing, and so he will place all sorts of things in the upper story.

Drawing upon his experience of working with many people in the 1960s who were taking LSD, Schaeffer suggested that for many, drugs were an attempt "to have a direct mystical experience that has no relation to the world of the rational."[44] As Schaeffer perceptively observed, the rationalistic, humanistic man began by saying that Christianity was not rational enough, but he "has come around in a wide circle and ended as a mystic—though a mystic of a special kind. He is a mystic with nobody there."[45]

Not only did Schaeffer reject secular existentialism, but he also had no time for its religious form. While he viewed Kierkegaard as the father of existential thinking, it was Karl Barth (1886–1968) whom Schaeffer blamed for opening the "door to the existentialistic leap in theology."[46] Although Barth held the higher critical theories that the Bible contains mistakes, he argued that a "religious word" comes through anyway. Thus "religious truth" is separated from the historical truth of the Scriptures, and as Schaeffer noted, "there is no place for reason and no point of verification. This constitutes the leap in religious terms." To Schaeffer, Barth isolated faith from reason, and his approach was merely "the religious expression of the prevailing thought-form of modern man."[47]

The appeal of Barth and neo-orthodoxy lay partly in the use of words that have strong connotations because they are rooted in the memory of people. Words like *Jesus*, *crucifixion*, and *resurrection* give an illusion of communication. Yet as Schaeffer pointed out, while one hears the word *Jesus* and acts upon it, the word is never defined.[48] The use of such words is always in the area of the irrational because "being separated from history and the cosmos, they are divorced from possible verification by reason downstairs and there is no certainty that there is anything upstairs."[49]

The New Thinking Spreads

Considerable space is devoted in *The God Who Is There* and *Escape from Reason* to explaining how the new way of thinking (i.e., the change of presuppositions and the leap from the lower to the upper story) spread by country, discipline, and class. Schaeffer noted that while it originated with the intellectuals, it was passed on to the mass of people who "received the new way of thinking through the mass media without analysing it."[50] He argued that BBC Television was "over-whelmingly" committed to the new thought-forms, and Christians were absorbing these "without being able to understand what is happening to them."[51] Rather radically for an evangelical minister, Schaeffer suggested that if he had to choose, he would prefer programs with swearing in them rather than those without swearing but that conveyed modern thought-forms. As noted earlier, Schaeffer contended that society in Britain had shifted from presuppositions that accorded with a Christian outlook as early as the 1890s.

It was not until the 1930s that a similar shift took place in America, and the middle classes were the last to change. As most evangelical churches were middle-class, evangelicals had hitherto been largely unaffected by the new way of thinking. However, by the 1960s there was emerging a new generation educated in the new concept of truth— i.e., no longer thinking in terms of absolutes or antithesis. Schaeffer realized that it was "not merely that they think different things. They think differently. Their thinking had changed in such a way that when you say Christianity is true, the sentence does not mean to them what it means to you."[52]

Taking the Roof Off

It was to reach such people that Schaeffer urged the church to teach and preach a clear grasp of presuppositions. He believed that "every person we speak to, whether shop girl, or university student, has a set of pre-suppositions, whether he or she has analysed them or not."[53] However, Schaeffer maintained that

> in reality no one can live logically according to his own non-Christian presuppositions, and consequently, because he is faced with the real world and himself, in practice you will find a place where you can talk.[54]

Interestingly, when Schaeffer started his ministry at L'Abri in 1955, he only thought that "most people" could not live consistent with their non-Christian presuppositions. It was the experience of dealing with the many individuals who visited L'Abri that led him to conclude that "no one" can live according to the logical conclusions of their non-Christian presuppositions.[55] This meant that "there is common ground between the Christian and the non-Christian because regardless of a man's system, he has to live in God's world."[56] Thus communication is possible and the gospel can be shared once the person is able to understand it.

Christianity, Schaeffer argued, is "the truth of what is there" in terms of the external world with its structures and those things within man that form his "mannishness" (i.e., his longing for significance, love, and beauty).[57] To deny Christianity and live on the basis of non-Christian presuppositions is to stray from reality, and the "more logical a man who holds a non-Christian position is to his own presuppositions, the further he is from the real world."[58] Schaeffer encouraged Christians to take into account the presuppositions of the non-Christian and push "him towards the logic of his position in the area of his own real interests."[59] As already mentioned, non-Christians do not live in consistency with their own presuppositions, and so there is within every person a "point of tension." Schaeffer held that each person "built a roof over his head to shield himself at the point of tension." Engaging in one-to-one apologetics affords the Christian the opportunity to find the non-Christian's point of tension and then lift his roof off. This allows "the truth of the external world and of what man is to beat upon him. When the roof is off, each man must stand naked and wounded before the truth of what is."[60]

Taking the person's "roof off" and pushing him "off his false balance" would cause him pain. Schaeffer believed that the Christian must constantly remind himself or herself that this is not a game to be played, and the person with whom you are in conversation must be able to feel that you care for him or her. Otherwise, Schaeffer recognized, "I will only end up destroying him, and the cruelty and ugliness of it all will destroy me as well."[61] Thus it was important not to push a person any further than was necessary for him or her to see his or her need of the gospel. Schaeffer strongly believed that the first truth to be shared once a person's roof is off is "not a dogmatic statement of the truth of the Scriptures, but the truth of the external world and the truth of what man himself is." This shows a person his or her need, and you then can share from Scripture "the real nature of his lostness and the answer to it."[62]

Modern man hardly ever considers himself to be guilty, but he often acknowledges that he is dead, and for Schaeffer, that was the place to begin. While the Christian apologist is to begin with the lostness with which a person wrestles, the task is also "to tell him that the present death he knows is moral death and not just metaphysical lostness, and then to tell him God's solution."[63] Schaeffer recognized that it often took much more time to press a person to his or her point of tension than it did to give him or her the Christian answer. However, in contrast to many evangelicals who would invite a person to "accept Jesus Christ as Savior," he stressed that the first part of the gospel to be shared is the truth that "God is there." Only then, he believed, was the modern person ready to hear God's solution for his or her "moral dilemma in the substitutionary work of Christ in history."[64] Yet Schaeffer rejoiced that when a modern person reaches this point and sees his or her need, no matter how complicated he or she may be in his or her thinking under "the line of despair," "the good news is the same as it had always been" and can be expressed in the same words to all people.[65]

A PERSONAL UNIVERSE

To help Christians communicate with modern persons and bring them to the point where they could grasp their need of the gospel, Schaeffer presented in *He Is There and He Is Not Silent* a cumulative argument for God's existence. Starting with Sartre who said that the basic philosophical problem is that there is something rather than nothing, Schaeffer sought to explore the problem of metaphysics—the existence of Being—and to consider the dilemma of man who has no meaning. If the universe had an impersonal beginning, everything, including man, must be explained in terms of the impersonal plus time plus chance, and this, Schaeffer contends, could not explain the personality of man.[66] Although all forms of determinism say man is not personal, Schaeffer believed he *is* personal and, while finite, is different from non-man. Mankind has what Schaeffer termed an essential "mannishness" (i.e., a longing for significance, love, and beauty), and this can be traced "through all the years, back to the cave paintings."[67]

For Schaeffer, the answer was a universe with a personal beginning, and for this to have an adequate basis there must be a "personal-infinite God and a personal unity and diversity in God . . . and Christianity has this in the Trinity."[68] To Schaeffer the Christian doctrine of the Trinity was a "reasonable explanation," and he even thought that without "the high order of personal unity and diversity as given in the Trinity, there are no answers."[69] Because this was the only answer to the question of existence (i.e., to man's being finite and yet personal), Schaeffer felt that "we may hold our Christianity with intellectual integrity."[70]

If a person refuses to accept that the universe had a personal beginning, then he or she has to face the problem that with an impersonal beginning, morals really do not exist as morals. Schaeffer maintained that "we can talk about what is antisocial, or what society does not like, or even what I do not like, but we cannot talk about what is really right and what is really wrong."[71] In an impersonal universe there is no standard that gives final meaning to such words as *right* and *wrong*. Yet the reality of life demonstrates that all people have what Schaeffer termed "moral motions." That is, people have always felt that there is a difference between right and wrong. When Schaeffer talked about all people having moral motions, he meant "all people," including the prostitute on the street who has her own sense of right and wrong.[72]

MORALITY THROUGH REVELATION

The question of morals also raised the dilemma of man: to explain his wonder and nobility *and* the problem of his horrible cruelty. Schaeffer suggested that

> if we say that man in his present cruelty is what man has always been, and what man intrinsically is, how can there be any hope of a qualitative change in man? There might be a quantitative change—that is, he may become just a little less cruel—but there can never be a qualitative change.[73]

He contended that if there was to be a qualitative change, it could only be so if you accept that "man as he is now is not what he was; that man is discontinuous with what he has been." In contrast to the non-

Christian philosopher who regards mankind as normal, the Bible teaches that he is abnormal and that, as Schaeffer put it, there "was a space-time, historic change in man."[74] Arguing strongly for a literal Fall in the history of mankind, Schaeffer warned about those "evangelicals playing games with the first half of Genesis. But if you remove a true, historic, space-time Fall, the answers do not exist." Given that man has true moral guilt, he needs a solution for it, and "it is here that the substitutionary, propitiatory death of Christ is needed and fits in."[75]

Schaeffer was realistic enough to recognize that some people would be unable to accept the biblical explanation and the Reformed position that involves verbal propositional revelation. However, he maintained that this resulted from their presupposition of the uniformity of natural causes in a closed system, whereby "any idea of revelation becomes nonsense."[76] In both *The God Who Is There* and *Escape from Reason* there was an underlying concern for the issue of knowledge, and in *He Is There and He Is Not Silent* Schaeffer dealt directly with epistemology.[77] During the 1960s while many evangelical preachers regarded drugs or sexual immorality as the major problems to be tackled, Schaeffer argued that epistemology was the "central problem of our generation."[78] It was a radical position to take up, and instead of appearing judgmental by criticizing the symptoms of the problem, Schaeffer went for the source: bad epistemology. It allowed him to come alongside those beyond the church who had been influenced by the new way of thinking. Schaeffer's approach also reflected his conviction that you are what you think: change wrongful thinking, and wrongful living will be changed.

Schaeffer encouraged non-Christians to consider whether divine revelation was acceptable or "even reasonable, not upon the basis of the Christian faith, but upon the basis of what we know concerning man and the universe as it is."[79] Drawing upon the work of secular anthropologists who say that they do not know why man should be a verbalizer, Schaeffer asked:

[W]ould it be unlikely that this personal God who is there and made man in His own image as a verbalizer, in such a way that he can communicate horizontally to other men on the basis of propositions and

languages . . . would communicate to man on the basis of propositions? The answer is, no.[80]

Unlike other Christian apologists who said people must "presuppose" the Bible as God's authoritative revelation, Schaeffer used less
dogmatic language. He just asked "why would it be unthinkable," he
invited people to "just suppose," and he suggested that "there is no reason why He could not communicate."[81]

TRUTH FOR LIFE

Schaeffer also argued that it would be very strange if God gave "religious
truth" in a book in which the "whole structural framework, implicitly
and explicitly, is historic, and yet that history be false or confused."[82] A
strong supporter of biblical inerrancy, Schaeffer contended for a revelation that was without error in all that it affirms.[83] Because the revelation
of God in Scripture looked outward to the Christ who died in history
upon the cross, Schaeffer accepted that this made the "Christian faith
open to discussion and verification."[84] He believed that in the Bible you
have two things: the didactic teaching of Scripture and also that "which
makes us say, 'Yes, God works that way.'"[85] In other words, what God
does in history and in the cosmos never violates what He tells us in His
Word. In reply to the despair and cynicism of modern man, Schaeffer
argued that Christianity had the answer, and he noted that

> the strength of the Christian system—the acid test of it—is that
> everything fits under the apex of the existing, infinite-personal God,
> and it is the only system in the world where this is true. No other sys-
> tem has an apex under which everything fits. That is why I am a
> Christian and no longer an agnostic.[86]

Seeing people come to accept Jesus Christ as their Lord and Savior
was for Schaeffer, as stated at the beginning of this chapter, what
Christian apologetics was all about. He was not interested in changing
Christian teaching in order to "make it more palatable" to the modern
person but in communicating the gospel "so that it is understood."[87]

Certainly his ministry at L'Abri is proof that Francis Schaeffer was a highly effective apologist who succeeded in helping many young people grasp the truth of the gospel and receive that truth into their hearts. For Schaeffer a person did not become a Christian by just giving mental assent to certain truth-claims but by entering into a personal relationship with the God who is there. Nor did he teach that this relationship is to be understood only in terms of the once-for-all act of justification, important though that is. Schaeffer gave equal stress to the importance of a "continuing moment-by-moment proper relationship with the God who exists."[88] In his other writings, and in particular in *True Spirituality*, Schaeffer explained how a Christian should live out his or her life. However, it is important to note that even an apologetical book like *The God Who Is There* called people to a Christianity that not only speaks of the truth but "also exhibit[s] that it is not just a theory."[89]

No Grand Plan

The enormous success of his three books published between 1968 and 1972 meant that the apologetical arguments of Francis Schaeffer reached a much wider audience than he had ever dreamed of. However, for many people this was their only contact with him, and some tended to either emulate him or criticize him solely in relation to these books. In particular, many came to view Schaeffer primarily in terms of the importance he accorded rationality in these three books. Conscious of this, Schaeffer added an appendix to later editions of *The God Who Is There* in which he stated that he did not believe that "there is any one apologetic which meets the needs of all people." Nor did he believe that what he wrote "should ever be applied mechanically as a set formula."[90] Indeed, it is important that we grasp that for Schaeffer *how* apologetics was conducted was as important as *what* was being said. For while Schaeffer is best known through his books, writing was never at the center of his ministry. His books on apologetics and evangelism emerged thirteen years after he had been conducting an apologetical ministry at L'Abri. To understand Francis Schaeffer's apologetics, it is essential that we consider the way in which he carried out his ministry. Without doubt, his approach was as much a part of his apologetics as was his argumentation.

The core of his ministry at L'Abri consisted of personal conversations with the individuals who visited it, and from these various conversations evolved his writings. Following his spiritual crisis in 1951 and his self-imposed isolation in the Swiss Alps, Schaeffer was convinced that his calling was to help provide a demonstration of the reality of God's existence. This led to Schaeffer's decision to live by faith, to make himself available to whoever visited L'Abri, to listen carefully and then give some answers to those seeking "honest answers to life's deepest questions."[91] A tape of these discussions and of his lectures to students at L'Abri developed gradually, and the book program (which started in 1968) came into being without conscious planning. Many of his books were based on transcripts of lectures he gave to Christian students in British and American universities and that had been captured on audiotape. And these lectures were in themselves the product of his discussions and lectures at L'Abri.

Thus while *The God Who Is There* is generally regarded as having emerged from lectures he gave in America during 1965, much of the material had already been worked out by him in 1963 when he addressed students at L'Abri.[92] And the ideas expressed in that 1963 lecture drew directly from his discussions with individual visitors to L'Abri. There was no grand strategy in Schaeffer's ministry, for everything was allowed to develop in a relatively haphazard way, and this reflected his view that quietness and peace before God are more important than any influence a ministry, position, or activity may seem to give. He warned that a Christian group "can become activistic and take on responsibilities God has not laid upon it."[93] Schaeffer's great concern was not to build an empire but to help the individual, and central to the work at L'Abri was a "personal compassion, based on careful and sympathetic listening."[94] As Colin Duriez has observed, Schaeffer's apologetics "was shaped in this context and hence was person-centred."[95]

LEARNING THE LANGUAGE

To communicate effectively, Schaeffer argued that the Christian apologist "must take time and trouble to learn our hearers' use of language so that they understand what we intend to convey."[96] Just as missionaries have to learn the language of the indigenous people they seek to reach, so the Christian church of each generation had to communicate in each setting the gospel with regard to "the language and thought-forms of that setting."[97] To those who criticized his apologetics and suggested that he just preach the "simple gospel," Schaeffer replied that you have to preach the simple gospel so that it is simple to the person to whom you are talking or it is no longer simple. He asked his evangelical critics, "Why have we as Christians gone on saying the great truths that nobody understands? Why do we keep talking to ourselves, if men are lost and we say we love them?"[98] Thus he suggested that

> if the word (or phrase) we are in the habit of using is no more than an orthodox evangelical cliché which has become a technical term among Christians, then we should be willing to give it up when we step outside our own narrow circle and talk to the people around us.[99]

Indeed Schaeffer argued that modern man does not even fully understand terms like *salvation* and *guilt*. He felt that when modern man thinks he needs salvation, "usually he is not thinking of salvation from moral guilt but rather relief from psychological guilt feelings."[100] Thus he was concerned that "many men who make a profession go away still unsaved, having not heard one word of the real gospel because they have filtered the message through their own thought forms and their own intellectual framework."[101] Schaeffer believed that much evangelism failed because Christians "had not taken enough time with pre-evangelism."[102] He indicated that if he only had an hour to talk to someone about the gospel, he would spend forty-five minutes showing him his real dilemma—that "he is morally dead because he is separated from the God who exists. Then I would take ten or fifteen minutes to tell him the gospel."[103] Schaeffer maintained that it takes a long time to bring a truly modern man "to the place where he understands the negative." But "unless he understands what is wrong, he will not be ready to listen to and understand the positive."[104] For Schaeffer this was best done through personal conversations because "each person must be dealt with as an individual, not as a case or statistic or machine."[105]

A REVOLUTIONARY APPROACH

Schaeffer's approach was quite revolutionary. It is important that we do not miss this. Not only was he urging evangelicals to be willing to give up cherished phrases so that the truth of the gospel could be communicated to those beyond the church, but he was talking about evangelism failing. For many evangelicals, the gospel was such a timeless truth that there should be no change in how it was presented. And given that the regeneration of a person flows from the sovereign work of the Holy Spirit, you could not talk in terms of evangelism "failing." Schaeffer's call for changes in language and style of evangelism (or at least, pre-evangelism) was strongly criticized by some. Some like Carl McIntire, Schaeffer's one-time friend and mentor, argued that all you had to do was "to bring conviction to these sinners in our modern day, preach them under conviction and then change them."[106] But it was not only the fundamentalists who disagreed with Schaeffer's approach. Dr. Martyn Lloyd-Jones, a leading figure in British evangelicalism and someone with whom Schaeffer still enjoyed friendly relations, remained unconvinced about the value of apologetics.[107] For Lloyd-Jones "there is no neutral point at which the Christian and the non-Christian can meet," and what the non-Christian "needs above everything else is to be humbled."[108] Without criticizing Schaeffer by name, he opposed any debate or discussion with non-Christians that afforded them equal standing. Speaking in 1969 at Westminster Theological Seminary, Lloyd-Jones declared:

> Truth is revealed to us in the Scriptures and by the illumination that the Holy Spirit alone can produce. I argue therefore that this whole notion of having a debate or a discussion or exchange of views concerning these matters is something that is contrary to the very character and nature of the Gospel itself.[109]

Schaeffer's approach to apologetics in the 1950s and 1960s was ground-breaking. While Lloyd-Jones maintained that people can be brought "to a knowledge of the truth" by "preaching alone,"[110] Schaeffer was attempting to explain the objective truth of Christianity through individual conversations and group discussions. Like any pioneer, Schaeffer's approach was vulnerable to misunderstanding. However, it must never be thought that the style of apologetics he developed indicated that he had lost confidence in either Scripture or preaching. Schaeffer, as we discussed in the previous section, was—and remained—firmly committed to the inerrancy of the Bible.[111] Nor did he ever abandon his preaching ministry. Sunday by Sunday he continued to teach the Bible in the Chapel at L'Abri. From the earliest days when he conducted Sunday services in Lausanne and in Chalet les Mélezes and had only his family or a couple of visitors for a congregation, Schaeffer preached a sermon.[112] Individual conversations and group discussions or lectures were always conducted alongside his preaching ministry. Yet, as Schaeffer said to the workers at L'Abri, he believed in the right of the non-Christian to ask questions and to probe the truthfulness of Christianity.[113]

FALLING ON DEAF EARS

Schaeffer recognized that all people, whether they realize it or not, function within a framework of some concept of truth. For him, the chasm between the generations was brought about "almost entirely by a change in the concept of truth."[114] Thus the Church was failing to communicate Christian truth to the next generation. Following a visit to the United States in late 1963, Schaeffer became convinced that this was the "greatest problem" facing evangelicalism and felt that there was "a specific danger of even the believer's children being thrown away."[115] He argued that if Christians were to be truly prophetic, they must be the interpreters of the world and "speak to the 'worldlings' and cause them to understand."[116] This conviction underlay his discussions with individuals, and it was his great desire to communicate "the gospel to the present generation in terms that they can understand."[117] Schaeffer deplored those evangelicals who, in their desire to communicate Christianity, were "tending to change what must remain unchangeable." Although firmly committed to the unchangeable truths of Christianity, he maintained that evangelical Christians must grasp what is "the present ebb and flow of thought-forms" because otherwise the "unchangeable principles of Christianity will fall on deaf ears."[118]

Yet it was this sort of comment that "raised eyebrows" within evangelicalism. When he visited England in 1963 he was challenged about his Reformed credentials by one person who asked him whether he believed "that if a man is of the Elect, he will hear the gospel so that he can understand it?" While Schaeffer answered "yes," he also stated that election does not remove from the Christian a "responsibility in communicating the gospel." Another critic in England advised Schaeffer not to worry too much about the problem of communication, for "when revival comes, the Holy Spirit will break through into history and then men will understand." Again while Schaeffer agreed with the truth about the role of the Holy Spirit, he argued that this "doesn't touch our problem of communication and our responsibility."[119] He longed for the method of explaining the gospel, as well as the message itself, to be suitable for communicating "into a changing historical situation."[120]

Schaeffer certainly gave greater attention to human responsibility for communicating the gospel than other Reformed writers did. Lloyd-Jones, for example, rejected the view that the modern person must be allowed the opportunity to have his or her say and maintained that "true preaching" would still draw people. He argued that "not to believe this is indicative, ultimately, of the fact that we have very little place for the Holy Spirit and His work in our outlook."[121] Yet Schaeffer recognized that you could not "separate true apologetics from the work of the Holy Spirit, nor from a living relationship in prayer to the Lord on the part of the Christian."[122] He saw no contradiction between praying with expectancy for a person and giving good and necessary answers to the questions raised by the person. In fact, he stressed that "we must consciously pray for the Lord's work as these adequate answers are given."[123] Schaeffer did not lose sight of the purpose of apologetics. For him it was "not just to win an argument or a discussion, but that the people with whom we are in contact may become Christians and then live under the Lordship of Christ in the whole spectrum of life." Nor did Schaeffer forget "that eventually the battle is not just against flesh and blood."[124] Despite the importance he gave to rational discussion and human responsibility, he maintained that

> as we look at the book of Acts, we find in the early Church not a group of strong men labouring together, but the work of the Holy Spirit bringing to them the power of the crucified and glorified Christ. It must be so for us also.[125]

SOVEREIGNTY AND FREEDOM

The balance accorded by Schaeffer to the role of the Holy Spirit and human responsibility in communicating the gospel was in some ways a more accurate reflection of the traditional Reformed approach than that prevailing among Calvinists of his generation. Perhaps in response to the emotional appeals made by many fundamentalists for personal decisions, the Reformed stream within evangelicalism had put such an emphasis on God's sovereignty that they failed to give proper attention to the human dimension. Schaeffer's approach was thus a healthy corrective. It also reflected his deep conviction that every person to whom we talk, "however far from the Christian faith he may be, is an image-bearer of God. He has great value, and our communication to him must be in genuine love."[126] Schaeffer frequently stressed that man "has not ceased to be man because he is fallen." Although twisted, corrupted, and lost as a result of the Fall, man is still man, and he "has become neither a machine nor an animal nor a plant."[127]

For Schaeffer the heart of the problem of modern man is the issue of personality and whether or not one lives in a personal universe. He believed that modern thinking viewed man as something determined by chemical, psychological, or sociological factors—a sort of machine. Schaeffer felt that "man is increasingly getting lost as he doesn't understand who he is" and is "lost among the machines."[128] It was to explain to the modern person who he or she really was, someone made in the image of God, that Schaeffer conducted his personal conversations and group discussions. Yet it was also because they were made in the image of God that Schaeffer believed that individuals could discuss the things of God. Schaeffer often pointed out that the Bible does not "reduce man to a zero," one who, incapable of doing anything, "just sits there and suddenly there is a strike of lightning out of the sky and he is a Christian."[129]

Furthermore, as people are created in the image of God with individual personality and are able to make a free first choice, they live as significant individuals in a significant history. An individual can choose to obey God or not "because he was created to be different from the animal, the plant and the machine."[130] In his many discussions at L'Abri, be it with an individual or with a group over the meal table, Schaeffer stressed time after time the significance of man against the prevailing secular notion of mankind as nothing more than a machine determined by various factors.[131] Although Schaeffer believed in unconditional predestination, he stressed that "history and humanity are not caught in the wheels of determinism."[132] Burson and Walls note that this emphasis is "an important thread that can be traced through the entire Schaeffer corpus." He spoke forcefully about the significance of human freedom "in order to challenge the ever-increasing mechanistic mindset of the twentieth century."[133]

LOVING EACH PERSON

To understand Schaeffer, we need to understand the love he had for the individual person. As stated earlier, he believed that communication about the gospel to a non-Christian must be made in love, for each person has great value because he or she bears the image of God. This was no dry theological doctrine for Schaeffer, who argued that "emotionally as well as intellectually, we must look at the man before us as our kind."[134] Each individual is unique and worthy of love, for as Schaeffer liked to say, "with God there are no little people."[135] Nor was this something he merely developed in the 1960s as an apologetical strategy to reach disillusioned young people: it was a lifelong core belief. Indeed it is crucial, if we are to gain an insight into Schaeffer and his apologetics, that we grasp the depth of his love for the individual. It was a belief that had not only shaped him but his entire ministry.

Back in the 1930s at a time when American churches sadly reflected the segregation of society, Schaeffer taught Sunday school to

African-American children while he studied at Hampden-Sydney College in Virginia.[136] In 1941–1943 he served as an Associate Pastor of a church in Chester that had five hundred members, but he found time to help "a child with Down's Syndrome, whose parents could ill afford special education."[137] People of whatever position or ability were important to Schaeffer and to his wife: they both believed that an effort should be made to make the individual feel special. For example, in the 1940s Edith had a cleaning woman who was African-American, and they had lunch together every day. "When they ate together, Edith put a candle in the middle of the table so the table setting would have beauty."[138] To Edith, the woman was not just the person who cleaned but a woman made in the image of God. This love for the individual underpinned Schaeffer's apologetics, and it was a love from which the apologetics sprang, rather than, as stated above, a strategy for successful apologetics.

In his apologetics Schaeffer thought that loving the other person as ourselves is the place to begin, though he warned that "genuine love, in the last analysis, means a willingness to be entirely exposed to the person to whom we are talking."[139] For the Schaeffers this involved opening their home to whoever was in need and welcoming whomever God drew to them, making it an issue of prayer that God would choose the people who would come.[140] We do well to remember that when L'Abri was established in 1955, it was not with the aim that it become a center for apologetics. The purpose of L'Abri was "to show forth by demonstration, in our life and work, the existence of God."[141] Thus the real basis of L'Abri was this desire to show the reality of God, and it was a desire that flowed from Schaeffer's spiritual crisis in 1951. Apologetics—giving, as Schaeffer put it, "honest answers to honest questions"—indeed became a key feature of L'Abri, but it should not be confused with its founding principle.[142] Apologetics quickly became an integral part of L'Abri, but this was not a distraction from its main purpose of demonstrating the reality of God. To the Schaeffers, living on the basis of prayer meant allowing God to "plan the work and unfold His plan" day by day rather than their deciding how L'Abri should develop.[143]

FROM SMALL BEGINNINGS

In some ways the work of L'Abri began even before Schaeffer formed L'Abri Fellowship and resigned from his mission board on June 5, 1955. The previous month Priscilla, his oldest daughter, brought a friend from Lausanne University who was struggling with spiritual questions home for the weekend.[144] Word spread among the students that Priscilla's father could help make sense of life, and more "young people showed up and additional conversations ensued."[145] L'Abri was run very much as an open home where guests joined the Schaeffers and were treated as part of the family. In a six-week period extending to the end of July, the Schaeffers had 187 guests who stayed varying lengths of time.[146] It wasn't only students who came to L'Abri: after the first visit in September by an American soldier stationed in Germany, there was a stream of GIs.[147] In the early days of L'Abri, Edith Schaeffer thought a full dining room consisted of about ten people, but by the 1960s she was providing Sunday meals to as many as fifty on a regular basis.[148] After Schaeffer's books were published, in 1968 the numbers visiting L'Abri really took off. One staff member recalls having to wash the dishes of 140 people who had been to Sunday tea.[149]

As L'Abri had expanded, other chalets had been acquired in Huémoz and more staff appointed to lead the work from them. These different households all formed a part of the L'Abri community, and while everyone would come together for lectures or church services, they normally ate in the different chalets. This, as Edith Schaeffer observed, "means smaller numbers around a table, gives opportunity for continuing the informal family atmosphere, and encourages conversation around the tables."[150] In addition to the chalets where visitors could stay, a chapel and study center (Farel House) were built as money became available. Farel House developed in response to requests from people who had been converted to Christianity at L'Abri and wanted to return and study for a period of some months. But those students who came to study at Farel House were not left to work by themselves through the extensive tape library that had emerged from Schaeffer's lectures and discussions. They were expected to take part in the reality of what was going on at L'Abri, including undertaking a share of the hard physical work (be that growing food or washing dishes) and listening to table discussions.[151]

FINDING A SHELTER

With table discussions, seminars, lectures on topics such as "The Intellectual Climate of the New Theology," and the presentation of papers by students, it was not surprising that L'Abri was described by *Time* magazine in 1961 as a "mission to intellectuals."[152] However, one would have a totally misleading picture of L'Abri if one were to view it as a place purely for intellectuals. No doubt some who have visited it, and perhaps even some who for a time worked there, would like to regard L'Abri as a sort of intellectual community. Of course, L'Abri attracted those who wanted to explore Christianity in more depth than the local church was either able or willing to do. Thus, as Pinnock has observed, Schaeffer was able through his intellectual analysis to help guide students into trusting Jesus Christ as their Savior and to help existing Christians to develop their faith in a more cogently reasoned way.[153] Nevertheless, we do well to remember that the number of people visiting L'Abri with purely intellectual problems comprised only a small percentage. The vast majority of those who came to L'Abri were young Christians who were just doing badly in their walk with God, whether as a result of drying up spiritually, being overwhelmed by personal problems, or difficult family relationships.[154] For them, L'Abri was truly a shelter.

For those who did struggle with intellectual problems—whether Christians whose faith was weakened by doubt or non-Christians who believed Christianity lacked intellectual credibility—help was not confined to rational discussion. Edith Schaeffer believes that in addition to long and detailed answers to their intellectual questions, something else was happening at L'Abri. "People were finding it hard to 'shake off' what they were living through . . . they were being given (not by us but by God's answers to prayers) a demonstration that God exists."[155] Deirdre Ducker, a former worker at L'Abri, recalls that "prayer was seen as absolutely essential, the mainstay of the whole work," for Francis Schaeffer "had instilled in everyone such a Biblical emphasis on the

Holy Spirit." Thus, for all the intellectual discussions, day-to-day life at L'Abri "was a visible walk with the Lord."[156] As Catherwood points out, love for the individual was a powerful demonstration of spiritual reality that "showed that Christianity was not just a set of correct propositions, but something true in experience as well as theory."[157]

LOVE AND COMPASSION

Schaeffer sought to show individuals love by understanding their experience and attempting to empathize with their plight. His compassion for the individual person led him "to tailor an apologetic strategy to each person he met instead of offering a canned systematic presentation or prepackaged methodology."[158] Those who worked with Schaeffer remember him as a man who had a genuine interest in the individual, who listened carefully, and who gave the person the time he or she needed.[159] Indeed David Porter, a Christian writer, says that he was won over by Schaeffer's attentiveness rather than by his arguments in favor of Christianity.[160] Schaeffer was a very emotional man who, as James Hurley witnessed, "often did shed tears of concern as he spoke with people. He was not speaking about a world of abstract ideas or ideals. His goal was to bring a message that would alter the lives of his hearers."[161] James Sire rates Schaeffer's compassion for people so highly that he suggests that it could almost be put "before Schaeffer's passion for truth and just after his passion for God."[162] That view is echoed by Os Guinness, who lived and worked at L'Abri for five years. He believes that part of the secret of L'Abri's success was that "truth mattered and people mattered."[163]

However, it is important that we remember that Schaeffer's love for the individual was not just a technique for successful apologetics. Rather, his approach to apologetics was successful because of his underlying conviction about the importance of the individual. Speaking of Schaeffer at the memorial service held for him in London following his death in 1984, Os Guinness said that for Schaeffer, "truth was personal because it was rooted in a personal God."[164] For the Schaeffers, loving people didn't just involve listening and talking with individuals, but, as mentioned earlier, it involved opening their home as an expression of love. Schaeffer was convinced that love was the mark of the true Christian, and thus Christians "must show a practical demonstration of love even when it is costly."[165] Opening their home and fostering a sense of Christian community was, as Schaeffer acknowledged, a "costly business." Everybody could come to their table, and "drugs came to our place. People vomited in our rooms . . . and we have girls come to our homes who have had three or four abortions by the time they are 17. Is it possible that they have venereal disease? Of course. But they sleep between our sheets."[166] As Edith Schaeffer recalled, their own "family life was almost non-existent," and life at L'Abri wasn't easy. "But we hadn't asked for ease. We had asked for reality."[167]

LOVE AS THE FINAL APOLOGETIC

Francis Schaeffer realized that many of the alienated young people who came to L'Abri were deliberately trying their patience to see if they would be accepted, and "when we pass the test we can begin to talk, but we have to pass the test."[168] Difficult though it was, and even painful at times, Schaeffer remained committed to reaching out in compassion and building a sense of community. He believed that "this is where we must begin. This is what the love of God means."[169] This approach reflected his fundamental belief that "true Christianity produces beauty as well as truth, especially in the specific areas of human relationships."[170] While the Christian's relations with all humanity were to be loving, his or her relationships with fellow Christians were to be "so beautiful that the world would be brought up short."[171] Schaeffer argued that one of the marks of the early church was a real sense of community that flowed from the beauty of relations between the Christians. This he felt was not exhibited by the evangelical churches, and there was a need alongside an orthodoxy of doctrine for "an orthodoxy of community."[172]

Indeed Schaeffer went as far as to say that the love of Christians "must have a form that the world may observe; it must be visible," for it is "the final apologetic."[173] Drawing upon John 13 and 17, Schaeffer noted that "Jesus gives the world the right to judge whether the Father has sent the Son on the basis of whether the world sees observable love among all true

Christians."[174] Living in an age that did not believe truth existed, Schaeffer asked Christians whether they expected young people to take seriously the truth-claims of the gospel if Christians did not practice truth.[175] Although he did not minimize the need to give honest answers to honest questions, Schaeffer also believed that "unless Christians love one another, the world cannot be expected to listen, even when we give totally sufficient answers."[176] At L'Abri, Schaeffer attempted to have a community that was in many ways a microcosm of what the Church ought to be. "[It] combines spiritual formation, intellectual stimulation, holy living, ethnic diversity, shared responsibility and mutual interdependency. It was a fertile context for engaging the whole person."[177]

CONCLUSION

With Schaeffer's concern for the individual and the importance of love as the final apologetic, it is not surprising that a regular visitor to L'Abri remarked that "most went away with the knowledge that they had been loved—with a sense of worth and a clear idea of the existence of God, and with the reality of communication on both a divine and human level."[178] Yet Schaeffer's apologetics have been criticized by Pinnock for being "preoccupied with rational methodology and propositions and inerrancy."[179] However, Pinnock fails to give proper attention to Schaeffer's approach and his method of conducting apologetics. I believe that this chapter has clearly demonstrated that Schaeffer's approach is as important as his argumentation. Any evaluation of Schaeffer's apologetics that does not give as much consideration to his method as to the message he shared is defective. As has been established, Schaeffer did not restrict apologetics to a narrow definition of a reasoned explanation but also applied it to how the Christian lived. Nevertheless, it must be recognized that there has been extensive criticism of Schaeffer by several evangelical writers in relation to the role he accorded reason. Donald Bloesch, for example, has accused him of having a bent toward rationalism for claiming that a person need not believe until he or she is "satisfied intellectually that the claims of faith are true."[180] We will consider this whole issue in the next chapter.

3

RATIONALITY AND
SPIRITUALITY

INTRODUCTION

This chapter will seek to evaluate what role Schaeffer accorded reason
in his apologetics and in particular to consider whether he gave it an
undue emphasis. The chapter will strongly argue that Schaeffer, when
understood in his polemic context and in the totality of his writings,
was not a rationalist. It does seem strange that Schaeffer, whose whole
ministry at L'Abri was committed to proclaiming the reality of the
supernatural aspects of Christianity, should even have to be defended
against charges of being a rationalist. However, it is the contention of
his critics that Schaeffer absorbed uncritically foundational
Enlightenment assumptions and thus that "a strongly rationalist spirit"
can be discerned within his apologetics.[1] It is certainly true that
Schaeffer attached great importance to rationality and so attempted to
show by reasonable argument why Christianity was the answer to the
problems of modern man.

The fact that Francis Schaeffer believed that the non-Christian had
the right to ask questions and explore the truth of Christianity is in contrast to the approach of Cornelius Van Til.[2] Those, such as Van Til, who
adopt a presuppositionalist approach to apologetics argue that "issues
between believers and unbelievers could not be settled by any *direct*
appeal to facts or laws because the criteria whereby we determine what

those facts and laws mean are not the same."[3] In traditional apologetics, the Christian had sought to find "common ground" with the non-Christian whereby they could meet in rational discussion (without prejudice to their own position) given that there are certain epistemological truths that are common to all people. However, Van Til maintains that

> it will be quite impossible to find a common area of knowledge between believers and unbelievers unless there is agreement between them as to the nature of man himself. But there is no such agreement.[4]

In contrast to Immanuel Kant, who said that we should completely ignore the demands of any alleged revelation external to ourselves, Van Til stated that the "very essence of knowledge is to bring our thoughts into agreement with God's revealed Word."[5]

As John Frame has noted, the "essence of Van Til's message is that God calls us to 'presuppose' Him in all our thinking."[6] Yet, it would be wrong to conclude that Van Til's approach resulted in him being unable to communicate with non-Christians. While he believed, as mentioned above, that the believer and unbeliever could not make any *direct* appeal to facts or laws, he accepted that in practice the Christian apologist could "place himself upon the position of his opponent" merely for "argument's sake." This allowed him to show the unbeliever that "on such a position, the 'facts' are not facts and the 'laws' are not laws."[7] William Edgar is correct to spot similarities between Schaeffer and Van Til in relation to their efforts to take "the roof off someone's house" and to place yourself "on your opponent's ground for the sake of argument." Nevertheless, there was still a distance between Schaeffer and Van Til and, as Edgar acknowledges, Schaeffer went farther than Van Til "in using this approach as a psychological device, digging into various tensions in the unbeliever's awareness."[8]

However, a more fundamental difference between them related to their understanding of the point of contact between the Christian and non-Christian. Unlike Barth, Van Til strongly asserted the reality of the point of contact, not as a common ground, which would only be a concession to human standards, but as revelation *in* every human being. Van Til's approach to the point of contact was, as William Edgar points out, "very carefully worked out and was meant to fit the rest of Reformed theology."[9] Indeed it was so carefully worked out that in the past I failed to grasp its nuances, and I am grateful to Professor Edgar for explaining Van Til's approach.[10] Van Til was concerned to find that in one strand of Schaeffer's thinking, the role of revelation at the point of contact was only partial. He felt that Schaeffer thus allowed unbelievers too much credence with their ability to make a proper use of reason. Because Schaeffer appeared to find the point of contact with the unbeliever in some area of interpretation of man and the world that the believer has in common with him, Van Til asked Schaeffer:

> Am I wrong when I say that you are, not merely for the sake of argument, but *in reality* identifying yourself with the unbeliever so that *together* you may discover *whether* the Christian answer is really a proper answer to your *common problem?*[11]

Schaeffer did not reply to the various questions raised by Van Til but instead continued to accept the right of the non-Christian to ask questions and probe the truth-claims of Christianity. Indeed it was this approach that led some evangelicals, as Louis Parkhurst has noted, to regard Schaeffer as a rationalist "because he tried to 'think with' sinners and appeal to their reason to convince them to accept with empty hands of faith the finished work of Jesus Christ [made on] their behalf."[12] To be so different from Van Til, whose presuppositional style has become the dominant school of apologetics among Reformed theologians, perhaps in itself makes some people suspicious of Schaeffer.[13] However, to view him as a rationalist is as much a misunderstanding of his apologetics as that by those, such as Steve Cowan, who wrongly view him as a presuppositionalist.[14]

FINDING COMMON GROUND

For Schaeffer, apologetics involved defending the faith against attack, and that meant giving answers to the objections raised. This was necessary if a Christian was to keep his personal, devotional, and intellectual life united. However, Schaeffer argued that "Christian apologetics is not like living in a castle with the drawbridge up and occasionally tossing a stone over the walls."[15] Schaeffer took it as a given truth that "no one can become a Christian unless he understands what Christianity is saying."[16] Thus for him, that meant a positive side to apologetics, namely, the communication of the gospel to the present generation in terms they can understand. Schaeffer sought to do that through his individual discussions, and in such conversations he held that we must allow "at all points" the person to "ask any questions he wants."[17]

Nevertheless, it is important to note that Schaeffer argued that there is "no use" talking to a non-Christian until his presuppositions are taken into account. Long before it was fashionable to critique the notion that you could enjoy pure empiricism and complete objectivity, Schaeffer stressed that there "are no neutral facts."[18] Drawing upon the work of Abraham Kuyper and Cornelius Van Til, Schaeffer recognized that everybody has a set of presuppositions, whether they know it or not. The groundbreaking work of secular scholars such as Michael Polanyi and Thomas Kuhn also helped him understand how all individuals interpret "facts" from a subjective basis. As Burson and Walls point out, Schaeffer was an influential popularizer of the valuable insight that "everyone views reality through a grid of guiding assumptions."[19]

Schaeffer was convinced that no non-Christian can be consistent to the logic of his presuppositions, and this provides a contact point. In 1948 Schaeffer had written in an article about apologetics that he believed that the non-Christian was "seldom consistent."[20] By 1963 when he gave a key lecture at L'Abri explaining his apologetics, he stated that his experience with people led him to conclude that the non-Christian was "never consistent."[21] Schaeffer argued that the non-Christian cannot live in consistency with his presuppositions because he has to live in the real world, and his or her presuppositions "simply do not fit into what God has made, including what man is."[22] Because non-Christians live partly according to a "worldview which logically can only belong to Bible-believing Christianity," their inconsistency creates a point of tension in their lives.[23] It is this point of tension that provides a point of contact between the Christian and the non-Christian. As stated earlier, Schaeffer did not accept that there are any neutral facts, and so he did not regard the contact with the non-Christian as "neutral." Nevertheless, he felt comfortable with speaking in terms of a "common ground."[24]

NOT JUST A GAME

For Schaeffer, finding common ground with non-Christians meant helping them find the place where their tension exists. He recognized that many people have never analyzed themselves, and so "it will take time and it will cost something to discover what the person we are speaking to often has not yet discovered for himself."[25] Schaeffer stressed that this "takes some love. It takes some thought. It takes loving this man. It isn't just cold, intellectual play with presuppositions."[26] Schaeffer's first move was to push the non-Christian toward the logical conclusions of his or her non-Christian presuppositions. He believed that the non-Christian enjoys a false optimism by living partly on the basis of Christian presuppositions. Schaeffer aimed to destroy that by pushing the person toward the despair and darkness to which his or her non-Christian presuppositions logically led. Rather than allowing the non-Christian to live in a halfway house, Schaeffer was convinced that we have to confront him or her with the logical conclusions of his or her beliefs.

> . . . you must take the roof off his house, and let the rain come in. You must take away his walls, and let him feel the blowing and the coldness of the wind—the wind of no meaningfulness, of blackness, the whole problem of being, and the whole problem of morals.[27]

As the "truth of his awful position" dawns upon the non-Christian, Schaeffer suggested that the Christian apologist should initially not make a dogmatic statement about the truth-claims of the Scriptures. Instead he or she should share "the truth of the external world and the truth of what man himself is."[28] Schaeffer argued that no matter what persons may say about themselves, it doesn't change the fact that they are made in the image of God. So "if a person says 'I am a machine,' he's still a man. He's still an image-bearer of God, even though he's lost."[29] For Schaeffer, this was "the key" to his work in making contact with the modern person who lived below "the line of despair." When a person comes to understand his or her true situation, then the Scriptures should be used to "show him the real nature of his lostness and the answer to it."[30] Yet Schaeffer recognized that even after the Christian apologist has exposed the modern man to his tension and has explained the biblical answer, he still may not be willing for the true solution. He sadly accepted that this would mean "we may seem to leave him in a worse state than he was in before."[31]

In discussion with the non-Christian, Schaeffer believed that the Christian should be ready to receive blows as well as to give them. However, while the Christian must take the blows of the questions that a person might ask, the apologist should keep pressing the non-Christian back, for "he must keep answering questions too."[32] Schaeffer's approach was very different from Van Til's. The latter argued that allowing non-Christians to use their reason in such a way will result in their assuming "the position of judge with respect to the credibility and evidence of revelation."[33] Van Til believed that only as you presupposed God-consciousness could you be "effective in reasoning with the natural man."[34] However, we do well to remember that Schaeffer did not regard the point of contact with the non-Christian as neutral, given that there are "no neutral facts, for [all] facts are God's facts."[35] Furthermore, we need to note that in his 1963 lecture Schaeffer stressed that the worldview or system of thought of the Christian and the non-Christian have "absolutely no common ground." Looking at the different worldviews from a philosophical point of view, he concluded that they were "absolute opposites."[36]

Schaeffer acknowledged that this appeared to be a contradiction of his seeking to find a point of contact with the non-Christian. His position is explained when we grasp his conviction that it would indeed be impossible to have a point of communication with non-Christians if they were consistent with their presuppositions. However, given that in reality no one can live logically according to his or her own presuppositions, "in *practice* you will find a place where you can talk."[37] In his 1948 article Schaeffer referred to this talking with the non-Christian as "a point of contact," but by 1963 he called it "a common ground." His many conversations with individuals at L'Abri led him to conclude that "there always is a common ground, not because there should be a common ground, but because, on the basis of the lack of logic of his presuppositions, there will be a common ground."[38]

With the non-Christian attempting to stand partly on the Christian's ground, the apologist is able to reach him or her. Schaeffer was able to differentiate between the theoretical (no common ground) and the practical (a meaningful point of contact). This shows him to be perceptive in his dealing with people and certainly not someone pre-occupied with any particular apologetic or theological system.

The Importance of Rational Discussion

Inherent in Schaeffer's belief that the Christian and the non-Christian should be able to question and trade blows in their discussions about life and its values and meaning lay a confidence in the rational ability of people. This confidence stemmed from his conviction, which he shared with Calvin, that the image of God was not completely destroyed in the Fall. It is a conviction we also see within Scripture itself. Paul, for example, is recorded in Acts 17–19 as one who "reasoned" (17:2, 17) and "tried to persuade" (18:4) and who was "arguing persuasively" (19:8, NIV). While the image of God was damaged in fallen man, for Paul it was clearly not destroyed. Schaeffer was concerned that "evangelicals have often made a serious mistake by equating the fact that man is lost and under God's judgment with the idea that man is nothing—a zero."[39] For Schaeffer, man was not only wonderful when he became a Christian—he was already wonderful by virtue of being made by God in His image. Thus he has value because of who he is by creation.[40] Because people remain God's image-bearers, they can assert their unique "mannishness." Schaeffer thought that the marks of "mannishness" include rationality, love, longing for significance and beauty, and a fear of nonbeing. Although a person is twisted, corrupted, and lost as a result of the Fall, he is still man, and as

Schaeffer pointed out, he can, for example, still love. "It would be a mistake to say that only a Christian can love."[41]

In the same way, Schaeffer argued that non-Christians can use their rationality to discover truth. Schaeffer maintained that through the revelation of the Scriptures God has spoken truth concerning Himself, man, history, and the universe. There is thus a unity of truth over the whole field of knowledge because God has spoken into every area of our knowledge. Nevertheless, it was wrong to conclude that because God has communicated truthfully, He has communicated exhaustively. Furthermore, given that the knowledge of mankind was not meant to be static, Schaeffer contended that man, with his rationality, is "able to, and intended to, explore and discover further truth concerning creation."[42] The marks of "mannishness" not only allow a person to discover truth about the universe but also to change something of its form. Drawing upon his or her rationality and beauty, a person can use his or her creative imagination to create and make—be it as an artist, a poet, an engineer, or a gardener—and so "change something of the form of the universe as a result of our thought world."[43]

In proclaiming the Lordship of Christ over all of life, Schaeffer was careful to teach that God has granted much freedom within certain boundaries. Referring to this as "form and freedom," Schaeffer taught that although God has created the form, which we—given that we are not autonomous—have to live within, He allows considerable freedom within that form.[44] This reflected his conviction that mankind remains "significant" and can affect his environment rather than be controlled by it as behaviorist psychology has taught.[45] Indeed Schaeffer felt that man has a "nobility," for there is "something great about man."[46] Thus he argued that one "must not belittle man's achievements. In science, for instance, man's achievements demonstrate that he is not junk."[47] It was this rational (but lost) man whom Schaeffer sought to reach with the gospel. Yet Schaeffer was not deluded into thinking that rationality was sufficient for salvation. He recognized that there is much more than reason and the intellect but stressed that "this 'much more' must be in continuity to reason and the intellect rather than in discontinuity."[48]

ANTI-INTELLECTUAL PREJUDICE

Schaeffer regretted that evangelicals "have been exceedingly proud in despising the intellect."[49] Indeed he lamented that many young people were not given any intellectual answers to the tough questions they were asking and with

> a sort of evangelical Kierkegaardianism, their parents and pastors patted the youngsters on the head and said, 'Don't ask questions, dear, just believe'. It was more spiritual to believe without asking questions than it was to ask questions.[50]

Schaeffer traced this anti-intellectual stance to the influence of secular Platonic thought, which he believed downplayed the importance of the body. This led to a tendency to view only the soul as valuable and to regard its value only in terms of its going to heaven and thus having "very little to do with anything in the present life—the body, the intellect or the culture."[51] Schaeffer, by contrast, argued that the biblical view was that "God made the whole man, and the whole man is important."[52] He therefore insisted that "it must be the whole man who comes to understand that the gospel is truth and believes because he is convinced on the basis of good and sufficient reason that it is truth."[53] Schaeffer recognized that being made in the image of God, men "have human hungers that need to be satisfied. To some the major need is intellectual; they must have answers."[54] Schaeffer was never foolish enough to believe everybody was a potential philosopher. But for those who grappled with difficult questions, his ministry sought to provide some answers.

Schaeffer realized that for many evangelicals who had been influenced, albeit unconsciously, by Platonism, their interpretation of 1 Corinthians 1–2 was adversely affected. They took its teaching about God having "made foolish the wisdom of the world" (1:20) to be an attack on wisdom and rationality as such. Rejecting this as bad exegesis, Schaeffer maintained that the biblical text showed that Paul did not despise the mind but was only opposing "autonomous intellectualism and refined contemplation."[55] Schaeffer acknowledged the danger of apologetics falling into proud intellectualism, but he also held that there is "the danger of lacking a love and compassion for man great enough to inspire the hard work needed to understand men's questions and to give them honest answers."[56]

Although rationality should never become "exclusively important" or be "the end of the matter," Schaeffer went so far as to say that "rationality is needed to open the door to a vital relationship with God."[57] As an illustration of what he meant, Schaeffer referred to the freedom an artist must have in creating a picture. Nevertheless, if there is no form to his painting, the artist loses all communication with his viewers. While it is possible to add to rational verbalization and so enrich it, it must be in genuine continuity with what has gone before it or "no one can say for certain what the added things mean." Rationality is certainly not the whole, but it "defines and provides a form for the whole."[58] Schaeffer hoped that the "biblical emphasis that knowledge is needed prior to salvation will influence us in attaining that knowledge which is needed to communicate the gospel."[59]

QUESTIONS AND THE HOLY SPIRIT

Schaeffer recognized that you cannot separate true apologetics from the work of the Holy Spirit and that there has to be something more than rationality. Yet he believed that man's reason was necessary to begin the process, and he declared that "if we give up the rational everything is lost."[60] In his apologetics Schaeffer wanted to "begin with man and what he knows about himself"[61] and the "present lostness with which he wrestles."[62] When through rational discussion you reach the point where the person is ready to hear God's solution, Schaeffer suggested that you just share the good news of the gospel. Once the person understands his or her need of salvation, whether he or she is a philosopher or a peasant, there is no point in being complicated, and "the same ideas and even the same words are all that is needed." Indeed Schaeffer frequently said to L'Abri colleagues that "everyone, in the end, has to go the same way with a double humbling as a creature and as a sinner."[63] For Schaeffer, his apologetics was not about changing the gospel in order to make it more palatable. Rather, its role was to overcome the "problem of how to communicate the gospel so that it is understood."[64] This is perhaps the key to understanding Schaeffer's apologetics and the role he afforded reason within it.

Not everyone whom Schaeffer helped understand the gospel came to accept it. Regeneration, the beginning of a new life in a Godward direction, remained the work and the responsibility of the Holy Spirit. But at least, humanly speaking, Schaeffer had done his job as an evangelist in explaining the gospel to the person and helping him or her understand his or her need of God's forgiveness. The experience of his own conversion to Christianity made Schaeffer sympathetic to those who wrestled with doubts and difficulties about the faith and who hesitated to believe in Christ. It was as an agnostic who wanted to compare Christianity with the claims of Greek philosophy that Schaeffer began to study the Bible. Over a period of about six months he became a Christian because, as he says, "I was convinced that the full answers which the Bible presented were alone sufficient to the problems I then knew."[65] While only a small number of people wrestled with the philosophical problems that Schaeffer faced, by the 1960s the majority of young people wrestled with the question of authority.

They were increasingly unwilling to accept authority or to believe something just because their family did or because they were told, without reason, to do so. Some of Schaeffer's most effective ministry at L'Abri was in communicating the gospel to rebellious and disillusioned young people who lived outside the reach of the institutional church. He believed that one of the key reasons he could communicate with hippies was the fact that he tried to get them "to consider the biblical system and its truth without an appeal to blind authority."[66] Taking time with the individual, giving serious consideration to his or her questions, and then presenting rational arguments for believing in Jesus Christ opened many young persons to the claims of the gospel.

Karl Barth's Blind Alley

Schaeffer totally rejected the neo-orthodox view of Karl Barth and his followers that it is "immunity from proof which secures the Christian proclamation."[67] For Schaeffer, Barth was only reflecting modern secular thinking in separating religious truth from the historical truth of the Scriptures. Schaeffer declared that man

> with his reason [can] search the Scriptures which touch not only 'religious truth', but also history and the cosmos. He not only is able to search the Scriptures as the whole man, including his reason, but he has the responsibility to do so.[68]

Citing scriptural grounds for this approach, Schaeffer referred to the Gospel of John (which was a record of signs so that we might believe) and the account in Acts 16 of the Philippian jailer. The jailer's question ("What must I do to be saved?"), Schaeffer argued, did not arise in a vacuum. It was because of Paul's preaching, the earthquake, and the way Paul and Silas behaved in prison that "the jailer had reason to be aware of the existence of a personal God."[69] Apart from the Bible being a revelation of God's plan of salvation, Schaeffer believed that it is also "true to what is there."[70] Thus as you read the Bible you discover that when God works in the flow of history, He works consistently with the way He says the external world is.[71]

In his book *Christianity and Barthianism* Cornelius Van Til wrote a stinging criticism of Karl Barth for being more irrationalist than theologically existentialist. This distinction between *Geschichte* (religious truth) and *Historie* (ordinary history or historical truth) led Barth to conclude that a "true faith will not build its house upon the quicksands of ordinary history." Thus he did not identify the resurrection of Jesus Christ with ordinary history and indeed said one cannot ascribe an "historical" character to it.[72] He was therefore quite willing to allow different interpretations to the resurrection and to other aspects of the gospel story. Van Til believed that Barth followed, without much alteration, the "type of dialecticism that we found in Existentialism and, back of it, in Kant."[73] As we have already noted, Schaeffer agreed with Van Til's critique of Barth. However, in his 1963 keynote lecture on apologetics, Schaeffer pointed out that by insisting upon the non-Christian's accepting Christian presuppositions before you can talk, Van Til "sounds the same as Barth." Schaeffer recognized that there were differences but suggested that *in practice* Barth's and

Van Til's approach were similar because "in both cases, there's no real discussion."[74]

In contrast, Schaeffer believed in the importance of rational discussion not only for explaining the Christian faith to others, but also for helping to ensure that the faith they express—if they come to belief—is real. Schaeffer maintained that since Christian faith is turned outward—to the person and the work of Jesus Christ—it is a faith that "rests on content. It is not a vague thing which takes the place of real understanding, nor is it the strength of belief which is of value."[75] For Schaeffer, rationality not only introduced you to the Christian faith, it continued to be an important element of true spirituality. He regarded 1 John 4:1-3, which teaches that a person is to test the spirits, the prophets, or any experience, as "very crucial in his own thinking." Testing a spiritual experience by relating it to the coming of Jesus Christ meant asking a question of content. And this is "a question in the area of where reason can deal with it." Schaeffer argued that the Bible teaches that "you must not trust the emotional bang you can get or any of this 'much-moreness'" but use what is open to you in "the area of reason and the intellect."[76]

RATIONAL OR RATIONALISM?

The importance accorded to reason by Schaeffer in his apologetics has been strongly criticized. Clark Pinnock, for example, has attacked Schaeffer for embracing a rationalistic apologetic that inevitably led him to "construe Christianity after the manner of a rational truth system."[77] Pinnock's criticism of Schaeffer is, at times, rather personal and patronizing. While commending him for what he sought to achieve given his "very unpromising background," Pinnock regarded Schaeffer as being much of the time "beyond his depth."[78] Pinnock rejected Schaeffer's claim that the Reformers shared his view that mankind, though fallen, is "not nothing." Far from accepting that Calvin and Luther endorsed rational apologetics, Pinnock argues that given their stress "on the witness of the Spirit to the Word, I think a decent case could be made out for the neo-orthodox interpretation of Reformation theology, in preference to Schaeffer's own rationalism."[79]

In view of our examination in Chapter One of Calvin's under-standing of our knowledge of God and the role of reason in this, we must question Pinnock's claim for Barthian neo-orthodoxy. With his strong emphasis on the importance of rationality, Calvin was no pro-ponent of a "leap of faith." By contrast, Schaeffer's "mannishness of man" finds a clear echo in Calvin's view that the image of God was not completely wiped out by the Fall. Given Pinnock's own sympathy for Barth, there is perhaps a large element of wish-fulfillment in his desire to claim an affinity between neo-orthodoxy and Reformation theology. Pinnock is wrong to say Schaeffer is "unfair" to Barth for failing to rec-ognize that the Barth of *Church Dogmatics* had moved away from his earlier existentialist theology of the Bultmann type. To talk of Barth, as Pinnock does, as "an ally in the work of defending the orthodox faith" is theologically incorrect.[80] Even in his later phase Barth continued to express solidarity with the concerns of existential thought. This is most clearly seen in his discussion of the philosophy of the French existen-tialist Jean-Paul Sartre.[81] As Cornelius Van Til has observed, Barth's approach in *Church Dogmatics* is basically the same as in his earlier the-ology. Everything centers around the idea of the Christ-Event, and in this God is wholly revealed and at the same time wholly hidden. From his consideration of Barth's writings, Van Til is convinced that Barth never forsook "his principle that revelation is historical but that history is never revelation."[82] In contrast to Barth, Schaeffer held that God had acted in time, space, and history, and so His actions were open to dis-cussion and verification.

Yet it was this very commitment by Schaeffer to rationality that Pinnock found so objectionable. He queried the very coherence of Schaeffer's basic approach given that he drew upon reason in his efforts to oppose autonomous reason and so position an inerrant Bible as authoritative. Pinnock believes that Schaeffer was so anxious not to view commitment to biblical authority as an upper-story leap of faith that "he saw it after the manner of a commitment to a rational axiom such as one would make in geometry. Such axioms are always chosen and then become the basis for subsequent logical deductions."[83] However, given that reason is fallen, Pinnock suggested that Schaeffer's argument lacked coherence. But isn't the question of coherence in itself an expression of rationality? Isn't Pinnock guilty of the very thing he accuses Schaeffer of, i.e., using fallen reason? Yet in practice he has no alternative, for rationality is in itself an expression of our humanity. Thus for us as rational creatures, reason—albeit fallen—is a functional necessity. Reason, while damaged by the Fall, is not destroyed. As Schaeffer often pointed out, "man is not only wonderful when he is 'born again' as a Christian; he is also wonderful as God made him in His image."[84] Schaeffer's use of reason does not indicate a lack of coherence in his approach. Instead it should be seen as a useful tool in allowing him to communicate with non-Christians.

RATIONALITY IS NOT ENOUGH

Schaeffer engaged with people in rational discussion, but it is wrong for Pinnock to term this a "rationalist" approach. Reason, for Schaeffer, is never enough, whether seen as the source of answers to mankind's deepest questions or as the sole guide to bring a person into relationship with God. Revelation from God and the illumination of the Holy Spirit remain essential: reason is never autonomous. Yet while Pinnock is wrong to depict Schaeffer's mode of argument as rationalist, he is correct in his view that Schaeffer has a clear preference for rationality as opposed to an empiricist approach. Many Christian thinkers find empiricism (i.e., the belief that all human knowledge arises from sense experience) attractive as they work out the details of the Christian worldview. Not so Schaeffer. He held that the presuppositions of Christianity and the alternative worldviews need to be considered to see "which of these fits the facts of what is."[85] Schaeffer did not present his presuppositions in a "straight authoritarian" tone but in a rational manner for discussion. Pinnock suggests that having put his axioms in place, Schaeffer, like Gordon Clark, "ventures out onto common ground with sinners and offers to debate the issues with anyone on the basis of the superior coherence of the Christian system as compared with any alternative world view."[86]

In the next chapter we will examine in some detail the status afforded by Schaeffer to presuppositions in his apologetics. At this stage we need only note that for Schaeffer presuppositions affected, consciously or unconsciously, how people reason, and thus they needed to be included in any rational discussion with non-Christians. Pinnock is right to describe Schaeffer's use of presuppositions as non-authoritarian; i.e., he did not simply declare them as absolutes to be received but presented them for consideration on the basis of their reasonableness.[87] However, Pinnock is wrong to view Schaeffer's approach as the same as Gordon Clark's. Clark attempted to show that all non-Christian worldviews refute themselves because they are internally self-contradictory. For him, the "ultimate test of truth is coherence," and he sought to establish that by the "application of the law of contradiction."[88] As has been observed, Clark "was undoubtedly the strongest proponent of coherentism among Christian apologists" in the twentieth century.[89] Gordon Clark is fairly unfashionable among many contemporary Christian writers who tend to regard him as a rationalist.[90] To be fair to Pinnock, I doubt that he compares Schaeffer to Clark in an attempt to label him a rationalist, albeit by association. Rather it is because he genuinely—but mistakenly—views them as being the same.

Coherentism, of the type favored by Gordon Clark, takes coherence to be both necessary and sufficient as a test for truth. Like Clark, Schaeffer believed that for something to be true, it must be noncontradictory, and he stated that we "must be able to live consistently with our theory."[91] However, Schaeffer did not view coherence as a sufficient test, and unlike coherentism, he also believed that the principle of correspondence is necessary to declare certain knowledge. We see that when he invites a person to choose between a Christian and a non-Christian set of presuppositions. Schaeffer asks people to consider the two sets of presuppositions and choose which "really and empirically meets the facts as we look about us in the world."[92] As has been noted by David Clark, because correspondence involves assessing "the truth status of statements by comparing them to the real world revealed through sensory observations," it is more empirical, while "coherence is a more rational principle."[93]

Although as stated earlier, Schaeffer may have had a preference for rationality as opposed to an empiricist approach, it can now be seen that he did not allow rationality a monopoly. For Schaeffer, Christianity was coherent, but it also corresponded to the facts of "what is." He believed that the Christian, given that Christianity as truth is comprehensive, did not have to choose between knowing the external or inward worlds. Indeed for Schaeffer the "strength of the Christian system—the acid test of it—is that everything fits under the apex of the existing, infinite-personal God."[94] The other key difference between Schaeffer and Gordon Clark that Pinnock fails to identify is in relation to the role of the Holy Spirit. Quite apart from the importance that Schaeffer attached to prayer as an integral part of apologetics, he gave a strong emphasis to the need for an increasing experiential relationship with Christ. Later in this chapter we will explore Schaeffer's teaching on a moment-by-moment spiritual reality. At this point we need only point out that seeking—in a personal and subjective way—the guidance of the Holy Spirit, praying for specific results, and relying upon the Lord to provide financial support was completely alien to the rationality of Gordon Clark.[95]

The Danger of Irrationalism

Whether in response to the criticism of Clark Pinnock or in reply to other critics, Schaeffer added an appendix to the 1982 edition of *The God Who Is There*. In it he defended himself against all those who viewed his apologetics as a form of rationalism, and in particular he refuted the charge of being an Aristotelian. He believed that they accused him of being an Aristotelian because of his emphasis on antithesis. Schaeffer rejected the view promoted by Martin Heidegger that rational thought in terms of antithesis originated with Aristotle. He maintained that Heidegger's claim lacked any historical foundation and argued that rational thought as antithesis is rooted in reality. For Schaeffer, "our minds are so created by God that we think in antithesis: so much so that the only way a person can deny antithesis is on the basis of antithesis."[96] Schaeffer understood salvation in terms of antithesis: he regarded the point of justification as the absolute personal antithesis. When a "person casts himself on Jesus Christ as Saviour, at that moment he has passed from death to life, from the kingdom of darkness to the kingdom of God's dear Son."[97]

Schaeffer noted that in modern theology there is no personal antithesis at the point of justification, for with the liberal theologians "there can never be a qualitative difference in man's relationship to God."[98] He believed that the writings of the later Heidegger were "crucially important in certain forms of modern liberal theology."[99] Thus by embracing Heidegger's upper-story semantic mysticism that seemed to give hope, modern theology drowns in a sea of anti-philosophy. Yet it wasn't only modern theology that was drowning: Schaeffer felt that modern secular man was left in cynicism if he didn't make some mystical leap. Writing in 1971, Schaeffer argued that positivism, which was an optimistic rationalism, had died, but the new alternatives "cause man to be hopeless concerning ethics, values, meaning, and the certainty of knowledge."[100] Twenty years before it was fashionable to talk about postmodernism, Schaeffer—with his lectures on Wittgenstein and Heidegger—was tracing fundamental shifts in the area of epistemology.[101] He recognized that some of his critics who accused him of rationalism did so because they had become trapped in irrationality and could no longer distinguish between rationality and rationalism.

For Schaeffer *rationality* concerned the validity of thought, while *rationalism* concerned someone beginning with himself and his reason plus what he observes, without information from any other source, and coming to final answers in regard to truth, ethics, and reality. Far from regarding mankind as autonomous, Schaeffer believed that his books stressed "that people have no final answers in regard to truth, morals or epistemology without God's revelation in the Bible."[102] Indeed one L'Abri worker has suggested that Schaeffer was so strong on revelation and the need for truth to come from outside us that he was like Barth with his emphasis on revelation. However, Schaeffer's theology of creation was stronger, and unlike Barth he was not afraid "to show a correlation between created reality and revelation."[103]

Pinnock claims that even in his use of the Bible Schaeffer acts in "a truly rationalist manner."[104] However, compared to the neo-orthodox approach to the Bible—which Pinnock finds so attractive, and which subjects Scripture to higher critical methodology—Schaeffer is distinctly non-rationalist. Nevertheless, one must note that in his eagerness to guard against irrationality and a theological leap of faith, Schaeffer could at times be overrational. For example, he rejected the idea that Abraham's willingness to sacrifice Isaac was irrational because "God's words at this time were in the context of Abraham's strong reason for knowing that God both existed and was totally trustworthy."[105] Yet this fails to deal with the point that when God initially called upon Abraham to leave his country and promised offspring to the seventy-five-year old, Abraham had no grounds to believe that God would be able to fulfill His promise. That he went to the land that the Lord showed him is indeed a testimony of faith.

WHAT WE THINK IS WHAT WE ARE

Meanwhile, another Christian academic, Richard Pierard, believes that Schaeffer's starting point—that people are what they think—is "far too simplistic." Pierard praises Schaeffer for helping him "to see that it was not necessary to abandon the life of the mind in order to be a Christian."[106] Nevertheless, he was unhappy with Schaeffer's stance that people's presuppositions determine how they act and, as these change or are modified, affect both individuals and the society they construct. For Schaeffer, what we think is what we are, and so he sought to persuade a person to embrace the Christian view of reality. Yet Pierard finds such "hard-nosed idealism" unacceptable and believes that Schaeffer failed to realize that "presuppositions are shaped by our cultural, social, economic, religious and political environment."[107] He felt that Schaeffer's philosophical idealism left him without many of the necessary tools to carry out rigorous historical analysis, and his "commitment to presuppositionalism places him far from the mainstream of twentieth-century historical scholarship."[108] For Pierard, opinion among mainstream historical scholars favored a theory that gave great importance to the social and economic conditioning of thought.

One has to ask why a Christian scholar like Pierard was concerned about Schaeffer (or himself) being placed outside the mainstream of twentieth-century historical scholarship. Why should Christians feel a need to find acceptance among mainstream scholarship, particularly if the presuppositions of that academic world are in themselves non-

Christian or anti-Christian? As Abraham Kuyper, the great Dutch theologian and statesman, has written, there is an antithesis between the Christian and the non-Christian worldview, and it is an antithesis that "is permanent and extends to every branch of scholarship."[109] Kuyper called upon Christians to wage a struggle against all compromises with truth in every area of life and learning. Much of the historical scholarship in the twentieth-century was Marxist-influenced, holding that "ideas change in accordance with economic developments."[110] The fact that Schaeffer chose not to go along with the Marxist trend in thinking was hardly grounds for criticism. However, it did mean that as he took up an unfashionable stance for truth he was seen as "Schaeffer *contra mundum*." Despite widespread admiration on the part of the general Christian public, Schaeffer stood increasingly alone, "not only against the secular world and the liberal religious establishment, but against many of the accepted leaders of evangelicalism."[111] Schaeffer's stress on the primacy of reason or thought might have been unfashionable, but it was not wrong.

Apart from rejecting the Marxist presuppositions that social and economic factors control the formation of ideas, Schaeffer's view that the motive force in history was ideas may have indirectly drawn upon the philosophy of idealism. Idealism, in its widest sense, held that the mind and spiritual values are more fundamental than material values. It opposed naturalism, which sought to explain the mind in terms of material things and processes.[112] Van Til, Schaeffer's onetime teacher at Westminster, studied idealism and "made liberal use of the idealist vocabulary (the philosophical use of the term 'presupposition' originated in idealism)."[113] Yet it is important to note that Van Til rejected the substantive content of idealism, and the most important philosophical influences on him, and also on Schaeffer, were distinctly Christian. It is therefore wrong to conclude that it was idealism that prevented Schaeffer from being able to consider factors other than ideas.

INFLUENCED BY OUR UPBRINGING

Pierard is completely wrong when he says Schaeffer's obsession with the propositional affirmation of absolutes gave him a "fear of sociological factors."[114] Schaeffer was quite capable of recognizing sociological trends—for example, the disillusionment caused by the Vietnam War and the protests against the "plastic culture."[115] Os Guinness, who was a close colleague of Schaeffer for many years, delivered a number of lectures at L'Abri that included a sociological examination without any objection from Schaeffer. Of course, Schaeffer rejected the sociological determinism of B. F. Skinner, who taught that all that people are can be explained by the way their environment has conditioned them. Schaeffer's position was "*not* that there is no element of conditioning in human life, but rather that by no means does conditioning explain what people are in their totality."[116]

Furthermore, given the impact of the Fall on each person, Schaeffer also accepted that there was, to some degree, a psychological influence on individuals. While rejecting the psychological determinism of Freud, Schaeffer recognized that all people have problems and that there are no perfect people, just "differences in intensity in psychological problems."[117]

Nevertheless, while recognizing other contributory factors, Schaeffer was convinced that in the final analysis it is ideas that drive and motivate people. On the basis of Scripture, he found wanting the sociological and psychological explanations for the moral problems of mankind. His exegesis of Romans 1:24 led him to conclude that it is not moral declension that causes doctrinal declension. Instead it was a "turning away from the truth—that which is cognitive, that which may be known about God—[which] produces moral declension."[118] Schaeffer called upon all Christians studying sociology, psychology, or ethics to resist the modern concept that all sin can be explained merely on the basis of conditioning. He believed that the modern secular explanations were not more humanitarian than the Christian view, for they decreased the "importance and significance of man."[119] Schaeffer maintained that the biblical view of mankind gives the person great significance. An individual "is not just the product of the forces around him. He has a mind, an inner world. Then, having thought, a person can bring forth actions into the external world and thus influence it."[120] By the standards of mainstream scholarship, Schaeffer's views on the primary importance of presuppositions may have been oversimplified and unfashionable, but they were biblical. Surely for Christians, that is cause for commendation, not criticism.

TOO LOGICAL AN APPROACH?

In his book *Francis Schaeffer's Apologetics: A Critique*, Thomas Morris asserted that Schaeffer's "argumentative progression and his terminology often indicate an underlying model of human thought or reasoning as a totally dispassionate, disinterested, nonpersonal, mechanical operation."[121] Morris felt that the weakness in Schaeffer's apologetics is that he failed "to recognize that predispositions as well as presuppositions must be taken into account."[122] Schaeffer's mechanical model needed, Morris argued, to be extended to include the many "tacit, personal, and nonlogical moves necessary in any process of coming to know or believe."[123] Some of Morris's criticism of Schaeffer may apply to those apologists who rigidly follow a presuppositional style. However, as Gordon Lewis points out, it cannot be said of Schaeffer, "the chaplain to the countercultural youth of the sixties," that he failed to recognize the importance of a person's predispositions.[124] Schaeffer himself stressed that apologetics should not be mechanical and that "each man must be dealt with as an individual, not as a case or statistic or machine."[125]

This personal approach to apologetics was appropriate, Schaeffer thought, because "the person before us is an image-bearer of God, and he is an individual who is unique in the world."[126] Nevertheless, Schaeffer was clearly concerned that those who adopted his advice about finding the point of tension in the presuppositions of the non-Christian were in danger of following a mechanical formula. He later wrote and added an appendix to *The God Who Is There*, stating that love should be the dominant consideration. Love and compassion were called for because the person is made in the image of God and is a unique individual and valuable. "Thus, we meet the person where he or she is."[127] As for the criticism of Schaeffer by Morris, Lewis believes that "in his entire book Morris makes no serious attempt to expound Schaeffer's views with any degree of objectivity."[128]

SALVATION AS INTELLECTUAL ASSENT?

A more substantial criticism was made by E. R. Geehan when he questioned Schaeffer's personal synthesis of theology and apologetics. He asked:

> Where does the regenerating work of the Holy Spirit fit into your apologetic method? In what sense is this divine work necessary? Of what import to apologetics is the doctrine of the Fall? How does the doctrine of election fit into a thoroughly rational apologetic for the Christian faith?[129]

Schaeffer knew that no one would "believe without a work of the Holy Spirit,"[130] and consequently that Christian apologists "must look to the Lord in prayer and to the work of the Holy Spirit for the effective use" of discussions with non-Christians.[131] Yet one can understand why Geehan would question the role of the Holy Spirit in Schaeffer's apologetic method. Apart from the above two quotations, there are no other references by Schaeffer in his three apologetic books to the work of the Holy Spirit in relation to a person being led into faith. The whole emphasis seems to be on the importance of rational discussion. In an important illustration about climbers being lost in the Alps, Schaeffer outlined how you would not blindly accept the advice of a would-be rescuer but "would ask questions to try to ascertain if the man knew what he was talking about and if he was not my enemy." In the same way, he suggested, God invites us "to ask adequate and sufficient questions and then believe Him and bow before Him."[132]

Schaeffer's illustration appears to suggest that if you can rationally establish a, b, c, and d, the person will accept e and become a Christian. At only one point in the Trilogy does Schaeffer acknowledge that the person "may not be willing for the true solution,"[133] and he does not explain why some accept and others do not accept the Christian faith. Neither does he mention about a person coming under the conviction of the Holy Spirit or deal with the place of contrition in salvation. All of this could lead one to conclude that Schaeffer was a rationalist, or at least gave an undue importance to rationality at the expense of spirituality. Indeed he even appeared to play down emotions or "experience" in a way that was alien to much evangelicalism that drew upon "German pietism and its emphasis on *Herzensreligion*, the religion of the heart." Tom Noble believes that for Schaeffer, trusting religious experience was "associated with liberalism, existentialism and subjectivism."[134] However, I wish to argue that Schaeffer was not a rationalist, and to suggest that he was—as Clark Pinnock does—only reflects a superficial and inadequate reading of him.

First, to deal with Noble's criticism, Schaeffer's alleged opposition to experience was in fact only an objection to locating the basis of truth within experience (which then had no point of reference). He also rejected irrational experience, which he viewed as a leap of faith in the post-Kierkegaardian sense. He believed that this resulted in a faith that was "introverted because it had no certain object, and where the preaching of the kerygma is infallible since it is not open to rational discussion."[135] For Schaeffer it was "crucial" that knowledge precede faith, and he argued, "only that faith which believes God on the basis of knowledge is true faith."[136] Nevertheless, and it is essential to grasp this point, Schaeffer did not view salvation and knowledge of God in purely intellectual terms. Speaking at L'Abri in the late 1950s he declared: "[W]e must jump the fence from where we are, if we have only believed these things as a sort of mental assent, into the experience and practice of it, and then we get hold of the reality of it."[137]

Schaeffer was adamant about the need for Christians to experience the reality of their salvation in the present moment of time. He maintained that without it, "our talking becomes just argumentation and unreal to us individually." Schaeffer believed that there "is nothing mechanical about the Christian walk, no way to quantify spiritual reality. It is always a person to person relationship in which we believe God."[138] Talking of Christ to a colleague in L'Abri, Schaeffer said, "Christ is the mysticism. The only mysticism with a base located in verifiable propositional truth which leads into a relationship which can't be put into words."[139] Schaeffer recognized that his own ongoing relationship with Christ could at times lack a spiritual reality, and so he unashamedly and "very movingly" prayed for a deeper reality in his life.[140] Hardly the approach of a rationalist.

Just as Schaeffer was not opposed to experience per se, neither did he reject a role for the emotions. While his public discussions and books presented an "intellectual apologetic," a L'Abri staff member noted that "in personal talks he often moved on to involving the emotions."[141] Apart from dealing with a person's emotional state, Schaeffer also saw a role for the emotions when a person accepts Christ as Savior. Although this is not necessary to secure a person's salvation, he believed that it is most helpful for a person to

> say thank you to God for your salvation. For so many of these new Christians, that's when the emotion comes. That's when they experience the reality of it. . . . That's when they have realized that it's really done, that they have really laid hold of the finished work of Christ.[142]

Furthermore, in his work at L'Abri Schaeffer felt no inhibition about displaying his emotions, be that in tears and grief for those he considered lost or in showing loving compassion to those struggling with problems. As Barry Seagren, a long-time, serving member of L'Abri, recalls, Schaeffer was "very warm" in his dealings with individual people.[143] When someone became a Christian at L'Abri, with joy Schaeffer would "crank up the volume on his record player, throw open the windows of the chalet, and fill the surrounding Alpine countryside with a vibrant rendition of the 'Hallelujah Chorus.'"[144]

SCHAEFFER'S POLEMIC CONTEXT

In *The God Who Is There* Schaeffer, as already mentioned, did not elaborate on why certain people accept the arguments of Christianity and others reject them. This has led some to believe that he regarded becoming a Christian as a human process in which the response can be understood in rationalistic terms. However, in the apologetics lecture he gave in December 1963 at L'Abri (from which part of the book was drawn) Schaeffer said that those who become Christians do so because

"God in his mercy deals with men so that they do accept Christ as Saviour."[145] Apart from this sentence the rest of the paragraph appeared five years later in his book *The God Who Is There*. In the 1963 lecture, which has hitherto not been quoted by any writers, Schaeffer referred to an earlier article that he had published on apologetics. It appeared in 1948, and he declared in it that in apologetics, people could not be converted "without the predestination of the Sovereign God." While the person converted is of "the elect," Schaeffer maintained that "election includes the means as well as the end."[146] Thus the rational discussion of apologetics was to be seen as an instrument used by the Holy Spirit. It is fascinating to note that by 1963 the reference to "predestination" and "the elect" had been dropped and that by 1968 the sentence referring to God's mercy in saving men had been cut out. Was Schaeffer becoming more rationalistic?

The answer is no, and the explanation for the revision appears to be quite simply that Schaeffer wrote and spoke with a particular audience in mind. In 1948 as a minister of the Bible Presbyterian Church he wrote for others from a similar background; in 1963 though he spoke to a group who were Christians, they came from a variety of denominations; and in 1968 the book was aimed at both Christians and non-Christians. Issues such as predestination were considered divisive, and as Mrs. Schaeffer later remarked, "because we are trying to do evangelism, we don't want to get sidetracked arguing issues that will prevent the gospel from being heard by the non-Christians."[147] Indeed one L'Abri worker has suggested that Schaeffer was adopting the "perspectability" approach whereby at certain points certain perspectives need to be emphasized though not given a higher importance.[148]

In his three books of apologetics, Schaeffer was anxious to present a rationally credible Christianity. By the 1960s it was widely believed among the Western intelligentsia that one had to "choose between treasuring our rationality and assenting to God's existence." Nicholas Wolterstorff points out that many theologians agreed "that believing that God exists requires throwing overboard the demands of rationality."[149] As part of his overall aim to win people for Christ, Schaeffer was prepared to fight on several fronts, and a key battle involved fighting the loss of rationality; so he shaped his writing accordingly. Even those like Pinnock, who criticize him for falling into rationalism, have acknowledged that Schaeffer "vindicated orthodoxy and put down liberalism in academically interesting ways."[150]

Taken in isolation, the Trilogy could create the impression that Schaeffer was over-rationalistic or at least gave undue importance to rationality. The latter point is explained by the above, while the former point is answered by stressing the need to consider the totality of Schaeffer's writings. As he himself often said, "An artist can't say everything in every picture but must be judged by all his work."[151] Nevertheless, even in *The God Who Is There*, Schaeffer makes mention of the "final apologetic" as being "what the world sees in the individual Christian and in our corporate relationships together." Alongside the rational argument, people must see "substantial healing" and so realize that "Christianity is not just a better dialectic."[152] He recognized that non-Christians could not look for perfection in the lives of Christians, but he felt that "they have a right to expect reality." For Schaeffer, the reality of our relationship to the Lord Jesus must be demonstrated in the present existential moment.[153] Thus I doubt if the Trilogy—even taken by itself—can actually be regarded as rationalistic. Yet there were those who did so, and to remove any misunderstanding, Schaeffer added an appendix to the 1982 edition rejecting the charge that he was a rationalist. Referring to the role of the Holy Spirit, he said, "as we give the adequate and sufficient answers (which we did not generate, but which we have from the Bible), we must consciously pray for the Lord's work as these adequate answers are given."[154]

A TRUTH SYSTEM WITH TRUE SPIRITUALITY

However, Pinnock would detect a rationalist influence at a deeper level within Schaeffer's thinking and in the very nature of his apologetics. It is this rationalistic mind-set, he believes, that led Schaeffer to construe Christianity after the manner of a rational truth system. It is certainly true that Schaeffer spoke of Christianity as a system and praised it for being consistent in a way that no other system is or has ever been. He maintained that as a system Christianity has the answers to the basic needs of modern man, and they are "answers which will stand up to the test of rationality and the whole of life as we must live it."[155] Yet he warned that Christianity isn't only a system. "God is there and we must be in a living relationship to him."[156] For Schaeffer, in considering Christianity as a total system, one has to start with the beginning that "God exists and that He is the personal-infinite God." He regarded personality as valid because it was rooted in the personal God who has always been.[157]

In a key address given in 1974 at the International Congress on World Evangelisation in Lausanne, Schaeffer declared that a "dead orthodoxy with no real spiritual reality must be rejected as sub-Christian."[158] This address was later published as *Two Contents: Two Realities*, and it has been described by one of Schaeffer's long-time colleagues in L'Abri as "one of the most important talks he gave."[159] In it, Schaeffer argued that the propositional truth of the Christian system must not be the end of the matter, as that would lead to a dead scholasticism. Instead, the end purpose of propositional truth was to enable us to be in relationship with God and to love Him with all our hearts and minds and souls.[160] For Schaeffer, this relationship involving our communion with Christ was true Christian mysticism, but in it "one is not asked to deny the reason, the intellect . . . and there is to be no loss of personality. . . . It is Christ bringing forth fruit through me."[161]

The book *True Spirituality*, from which the above quotation is taken, is the key to understanding Schaeffer, rather than the Trilogy. Although not published until after the Trilogy, *True Spirituality* was written as an outcome of his 1951 spiritual crisis, and it reflects the change in his life. Schaeffer himself regarded it as "the real basis" of L'Abri and welcomed its publication as a counterbalance to his three books on apologetics. While seeking to keep a balance between the intellectual side and the spiritual reality, he acknowledged that this was more difficult to do in books than it was in the community of L'Abri itself.[162] I believe that this acknowledgment in 1973 about the need for balance reflected his concern that some readers of the Trilogy—be they critics or followers—only focused on the rationality of his apologetics and overlooked his spirituality. As pointed out in the previous chapter, many people only know Schaeffer through his three apologetical books, and they view him primarily in terms of the importance he accorded rationality in these books. Sadly, they have not grasped that for Schaeffer *how* apologetics was conducted was as important as *what* was being said. Nor have some realized the spirituality that underlay the rationality of his apologetics.

THE NEED FOR REALITY

True Spirituality was a book Schaeffer re-read time and again. In it he says that while doctrine is important, it is not an end in itself. There is to be a "moment-by-moment, increasing, experiential relationship to Christ."[163] Schaeffer stressed that salvation, as the word is used in Scripture, is wider than justification. In the future there is glorification, but there is also a present aspect of salvation. Sanctification is our present relationship to our Lord. While there are no degrees of justification—once you accept Jesus Christ as Savior, your guilt is absolutely gone—there are degrees of sanctification. There are degrees between different Christians, and we must also acknowledge degrees in our personal lives at different times.[164] Schaeffer believed that the present aspect of salvation must be emphasized because "Christians are called upon to be a demonstration at our point of history that the supernatural, the normally unseen world, does exist; and beyond that, that God exists."[165]

As Christians live by faith, and as Christ brings forth His fruit in us by the indwelling of the Holy Spirit, the way is open for the individual Christian to begin to know in the present life the reality of the supernatural. And for Schaeffer, this is where the Christian ought to live.[166]

Schaeffer maintained that as Christians many of us experience a loss of reality in our Christian lives because we have lost the reality of the supernatural view of the total universe. Thus we "allow the spirit of the naturalism of the age to creep into our thinking, unrecognized."[167] Schaeffer argued that the true Christian life means living in the two halves of reality: the supernatural and the natural. For him there was a cause-and-effect relationship from the seen to the unseen world, and the real battle is in the heavenlies. Those Christians who do not live their present moment in the light of the supernatural, Schaeffer accused of living a life of "unfaith." He believed that they had reduced Christianity to a dialectic or simply a good philosophy. And while he agreed that Christianity is a good philosophy, he taught that it is not *only* a good philosophy, for Christianity involves how we live in God's universe.[168] For Schaeffer, truth, while vital for salvation, has to be lived out to be real. As he put it, "in the last analysis it is never doctrine *alone* that is important. It is always doctrine *appropriated* that counts."[169]

Schaeffer realized that if we try to live the Christian life in our own strength, we will only have failure and sorrow. However, he believed that we can experience great joy if we live in the power of Christ "through the agency of the indwelling Holy Spirit, by faith, moment by moment."[170] Schaeffer explained how, by drawing upon the reality of our relationship with God, we can experience a "substantial healing" in all our relationships. He was convinced, on the basis of biblical teaching, that perfectionism (i.e., overcoming all sin) is not possible. Nevertheless, Schaeffer believed that by taking hold of the spiritual reality, Christians can discover "that they can have in the present life the substantial healing of the separation from themselves that is a result of the Fall and of sin."[171] He maintained that this substantial healing applies not only to our separation from God but to the separation we experience from ourselves and from other people. In *True Spirituality* Schaeffer therefore devoted whole chapters to the substantial healing of psychological problems and personal relationships.

FOUNDATIONAL FOR SCHAEFFER

True Spirituality, as already mentioned, was only published in 1971. Yet the material from which the book developed was first presented in a series of talks in the USA during 1953, then was repeated in 1955 when L'Abri began, and was reworked in a more complete form in 1963. Following their recording in 1964, when the talks were again given, the material (in tape form) was made available for study to individual visitors to L'Abri. The tapes were widely used by the Lord, as Schaeffer observed, to help people with spiritual and psychological problems in "a way that has moved us deeply."[172] Thus it can be seen that a stress on the need for a moment-by-moment personal spiritual reality with

Christ lay at the heart of Schaeffer's ministry at L'Abri. Long before the charismatic movement burst upon the scene in the 1960s, Schaeffer was proclaiming the importance of living in the power of the Holy Spirit. Writing to a friend in 1951, Schaeffer remarked about the joy of being indwelt by the Holy Spirit and then added, "would to God that our ministry could be under His full direction, and in His power without reservation."[173] With the establishment of L'Abri in 1955, Schaeffer was anxious that his ministry, as much as his life, be conducted under the direction of the Holy Spirit.

I have dealt with *True Spirituality* in considerable detail because of its importance in enabling us to understand Schaeffer and to evaluate his apologetics in relation to the totality of the man. It allows us to see that Pinnock's claim that Schaeffer reduced Christianity to a rational truth system is incorrect. Not only did Schaeffer not allow rationalism to control his apologetics, but neither did he allow his apologetics to control his theology. It is quite simply not true that Schaeffer's emphasis on the inerrancy of the Bible led him "to inflate the admittedly important place of the Bible in Christianity and thus to obscure the very point of the Bible, which is to bear witness to Jesus Christ."[174]

In *The God Who Is There* Schaeffer says that truth is "not ultimately related even to Scripture" but "is finally related to something behind the Scriptures." For Schaeffer the final screen of Christian truth is "that which is in relationship to what exists and ultimately to the God who exists."[175] And once again Schaeffer stated that true spirituality consists of being in relationship to God. This involves, first, the "once-for-all act of justification, [and] secondly, . . . being in that correct relationship as a continuing moment-by-moment reality."[176] It is worth pointing out that the above quote comes not from *True Spirituality* but from *The God Who Is There*. Thus even in one of his books that gave an important role to rationality, Schaeffer gave the greatest importance to spirituality and the need for that to find a moment-by-moment reality.

SALVATION AS PERSONAL AND RELATIONAL

Burson and Walls suggest that though "Schaeffer places a heavy emphasis on sanctification and the relational aspect of salvation, he clearly gives justification the logical priority."[177] They also think that Schaeffer views the means by which we enjoy justification "primarily as a legal act of substitutionary punishment."[178] Although they do not accuse him of being a rationalist (in the way Pinnock does), by depicting him as understanding salvation primarily in terms of legal justification and expressing it in rational, doctrinal terms, they help create such an impression. However, they are quite wrong in their assessment of Schaeffer. Certainly Schaeffer believed in the utter necessity of a moment in our life when, by grace, we accept Jesus Christ as our Savior and are justified by faith before God. Yet he did not give it priority over the relational aspects of salvation.

Schaeffer spoke against the danger of "thinking of Christianity as merely a sort of progression, without understanding that there must be a moment of justification, a moment of birth."[179] Although this brings us within a proper legal relationship with God, Schaeffer pointed out that God's dealing with us is "not primarily legal" but personal. God Himself always deals with us on the basis of a personal relationship.[180] Justification is an essential part of salvation, but "salvation also includes certain ongoing realities in our present life."[181] It is true that justification comes first, but its only "priority" is chronological in that there is a historical sequence: first justification, then sanctification. Writing in *The God Who Is There*, Schaeffer stated:

> Birth is essential to life, but the parent is not glad only for the birth of his child. He is thankful for the living child that grows up. . . . So it is with becoming a Christian. In one way you can say that the new birth is everything; in another way you can say that really it is very little . . . it is very little in comparison with the living existential relationship. The legal circle of justification . . . opens to me a living person-to-person communication with the God who exists.[182]

Schaeffer understood Christianity in terms of three concentric circles. The outer circle is the apologetic and defensive, while the middle circle is the intellectual (i.e., the doctrines of the faith expressed in a positive way). Important though this middle circle was, Schaeffer recognized that if it stood alone, it was not Christianity. For him, that involved the innermost circle, which is spiritual (i.e., "the personal relationship of the individual soul with a personal God"[183]). Schaeffer deeply regretted that many evangelicals looked back to the moment of their justification as if that were the end of salvation, at least until death comes. When asked to give a word of testimony in church, he noted that many Christians spoke of their conversion albeit twenty or thirty years ago but said nothing about anything since. He believed that salvation is a running stream and not something static and warned that if we don't have something fresh to thank the Lord for today, we "have surely fallen into mere orthodoxy, with no reality to it at all."[184] To avoid this, not only should our relationship with God be real, but people "should see a beauty among Christians in their practice of the centrality of personal relationships."[185]

Schaeffer felt that there was a unity between the apologetic and spiritual writings that people needed to recognize. In the running of L'Abri he attempted to maintain this approach so that when "people come to L'Abri they are faced with these two aspects simultaneously, as the two sides of a single coin."[186] He acknowledged that the balance wasn't always totally kept but remarked that through prayer they consciously asked the Lord "for His help. And I think that is what all of us must do."[187] This brings us to the question of prayer, which Schaeffer regarded as utterly essential. L'Abri was built upon the concept of prayer, and it is very interesting to note that in 1964 when the community was growing, both in terms of numbers and buildings, Schaeffer gave a sermon series on the importance of prayer. As the new chapel opened and L'Abri took on a greater sense of permanency, Schaeffer called everyone in the community to spend time preparing their hearts and reflecting about their prayer life as he spoke on the subject.

PRAYER AND THE HOLY SPIRIT

On the first Sunday in the new chapel, he declared that too often Christians live "as if there was no promise of the Holy Spirit and as if the promises concerning prayer were simply not made." He suggested that if God withdrew the promises about the Holy Spirit, the "awful thing" is that it would make "no difference what-so-ever" to most

Christians. Schaeffer regarded this as "wrong beyond all words" in view of the emphasis in the Bible on prayer and the role of the Holy Spirit.[188] It was for him an example of "unfaith" when a Christian prays so little, because while such a Christian might claim to believe in God's supernatural world, he or she does not act in practice on the basis of the supernatural in the present life. For Schaeffer, prayer and the work of the Holy Spirit must be coupled together since Scripture reveals them to be closely related in a very special way.

Schaeffer believed that the Bible presents "a picture of prayer which is simplicity, practicability and power." Prayer is simply our speaking to the God who is there, and he suggested that our prayer life should be like those early disciples who knew Jesus face-to-face. In their relationship with Jesus while he was on the earth, "they expected to be heard and so should we."[189] By "practicability" Schaeffer meant that prayer has, among other things, a result in the external world. However, he recognized that the power of our prayer at any particular time rests upon our attitudes and the quality of our Christian life at that moment. Consequently, "not all Christians are in equal place and none of us are in equal place all the time."[190] If, as Schaeffer thought, prayer is at the heart of maintaining our spiritual reality and developing our relationship with God, then conversely our relationship with God is at the heart of our prayer life. Schaeffer understood prayer in a very relational way and compared our talking to God in prayer to a "little child with his hands up-raised saying to his father 'Up, daddy, up.'"[191]

In prayer, Schaeffer suggested, we should have the same attitude as a little child—trusting, depending, and longing to be lovingly embraced by our Father. Citing Romans 8:26, Schaeffer pointed out the role of the Holy Spirit in taking our prayers when we don't know what to say and making them what they should be. To people worried about selecting the right words, Schaeffer said, "it does not matter. If your cry is right, it is heard as it is really meant." Here is Schaeffer, the man accused by Pinnock of being a rationalist who is preoccupied with propositions, referring to our communication with God in a form beyond words. Hardly the rationalist! Quoting Gresham Machen, the founder of Westminster Theological Seminary, that there are times when we cannot even verbalize our cry, and all the child of God can say is, "Father," Schaeffer acknowledged that he had known such times. Yet because we deal with God, there is a "tremendous reality," a "tremendous power," and something "really happens." He felt that this explained why the apostles said in Acts 6, in the order they did, that they would give their attention to prayer and to the ministry of the Word.[192]

CORRUPTED BY THE FALL

One of the questions raised by Geehan concerned the doctrine of the Fall and its relationship to apologetics. While Schaeffer laid great importance on a true, historic, space-time Fall, it has to be said that he made very little reference to the noetic effects of the Fall in the present-time reality. Although (as a Presbyterian) Schaeffer believed in the doctrine of total depravity and recognized that the inherent corruption of sin extends to the faculties of the mind,[193] in practice this appeared to make little difference as to how he conducted rational discussion. Of course, he recognized the limitation of the mind and its inability to reason through to a saving knowledge of God without special revelation.[194] Yet Schaeffer remained confident that man's rational abilities were such that the Christian apologist could appeal to them. As stated earlier, because men were "not logical to their system, in practice you can find a tension and common ground: so you can talk in terms which can be traded."[195]

However, lest we conclude that in practice Schaeffer's apologetics accorded reason too great a role, we do well to remember just what he was about. Schaeffer was an evangelist who wanted to rescue the lost, and his apologetics was a tool employed in that work. Evangelism, not apologetics, guided his ministry. Working in the 1960s when academics regarded evangelical Christianity as irrational, Schaeffer was concerned to show it as being rationally credible. He was also anxious to oppose the mysticism influencing students exploring the Eastern religions. Schaeffer therefore gave an emphasis to the rational faculties and their role in our coming to a knowledge of God. This is an example of what Gavin McGrath has called the perspectability approach: certain perspectives need to be emphasized but not accorded a higher importance. Emphasizing certain perspectives and downplaying others was a common approach adopted by Schaeffer. To put an emphasis on the importance of rational discussion wasn't to imply that rationality was all-important but rather that it was most appropriate in that environment. In the same way, we can understand Schaeffer's lack of real emphasis on the need for personal confession and repentance from sin. It was not because he thought people were not guilty of sin, for after all, as already stated, he held that the central antithesis of the Christian faith is the moment of justification.[196] Rather, Schaeffer's not stressing the need for repentance from sin was a reaction against the "heavy emphasis given by some fundamentalists to repentance."[197]

In giving a certain emphasis to rationality, Schaeffer believed that what he did "was an application of what Paul did in Romans 1 and 2."[198] In the end non-Christians will be judged guilty because there was sufficient evidence for them to know the truth that there is a God. Schaeffer maintained that creation "reveals knowledge to the rational person—who can't escape his rationality even though he is a rebel."[199] In seeking to explain to persons about their need of God, Schaeffer was just attempting to draw upon their innate rationality. He held that despite the Fall, "man continues to be a rational, moral creature. He never becomes a machine."[200] Yet while Schaeffer may not have made many references to the sinful corruption of the mind, he recognized its limitations. It was not just that he recognized the need of the Holy Spirit to provide illumination in addition to rational discussion, but he accepted the need for the Holy Spirit to be working through the rational discussion. There is a tendency by some to isolate events—the discussion, the moment of conversion, etc.—but Schaeffer's approach was to see it as an integrated whole. He did not believe that you established by rational argument that Christianity is true, and then (and only then) did the Holy Spirit take over to lead you into faith. For Schaeffer there was "a constant interchange of faith and reason all the time."[201] It was never either/or; rationality and the Holy Spirit always interacted. Furthermore, the Holy Spirit didn't just engage the mind but also related to the emotions. The Holy Spirit did not only illuminate in order to give understanding, but He dealt with the noetic effects of the Fall.

Thus He provided "a sense of conviction and rebuking and a humbling of the mind."[202] While Schaeffer gave an emphasis to rationality, he never divorced it from the whole of a person's experience, nor wanted to promote intellectualism, never mind rationalism. As Ranald Macaulay, his successor at L'Abri, put it, their vision was

> a mind which is overwhelmed by the reality of God's truth, of God's Word, revealed from above, thrilled by its objectivity and its rationality, and as a result of that, in love with God, rejoicing in Him and labouring gladly for Him.[203]

Conclusion

While this chapter has demonstrated that Schaeffer did not accord reason too great a role, some evangelicals felt that the emphasis he gave to rational discussion was misplaced. Influenced by Abraham Kuyper, they favor a presuppositional approach to apologetics. As outlined in Chapter One, Kuyper held the view that God "as revealed in Scripture is known by us, not as a conclusion of an argument, but as a primary truth immediately apprehended as the result of spiritual communication to the human consciousness."[204] Perhaps it is because Geehan stands firmly in the tradition of Kuyper and adopts Van Til's approach that he is unhappy with the way Schaeffer seeks to use biblical doctrines (such as the Fall and the Trinity) to deal with apologetic questions. Geehan felt that Schaeffer should have mentioned that these doctrines "are conceptually elusive having long histories as recalcitrant puzzles within Christian theology."[205] As we have noted in this chapter, Schaeffer repeatedly emphasized that no one can fully comprehend God or His revealed truth. Yet, as Lewis points out, for Schaeffer "the mysterious is the incomprehensible, but not the illogical, the unreal, or the irrelevant."[206] Surely this is correct, and Schaeffer was right to want to demonstrate that "Christianity is not a blind leap of faith but rather that there are good and sufficient reasons which can be pursued with one's reason for knowing that Christianity is Truth."[207]

Nevertheless, Schaeffer recognized that there are certain things about God—such as the Trinity—that we cannot grasp. He stated:

[W]e must stop here where the Bible stops and as soon as we try to explain the infinite God with our finite knowledge we begin to twist the Scriptures and we are rationalistic in the bad and Enlightenment sense of insisting that we as finite can put everything into mathematical, Cartesian formulas.[208]

Written in 1981, three years before he died, the above letter indicates that Schaeffer continued to accord reason an extremely important role, but, as in 1948, it was a reason to be exercised within the limits set by the Sovereign God. It was a marvel to Schaeffer that God, who is infinite, should in His infinity "create significant people in a significant history."[209] Holding these two truths in tension—God's infinity and man's significance—is difficult, but Schaeffer was right to try.

4

ACADEMIC OR
APOLOGIST?

INTRODUCTION

Given that the previous chapter examined the importance Schaeffer
afforded to rationality and considered whether or not he was a rationalist, it is interesting to see him criticized for the inadequacy of his
argumentation. This chapter will explore whether Schaeffer was inconsistent in the way he used reason in his apologetics, and in particular
it will consider whether he relied upon a presuppositionalist approach
rather than attempting to argue his case. As Burson and Walls observe,
the "question of apologetic methodology is probably the most disputed
and controversial subject surrounding the life and ministry of Francis
Schaeffer."[1] I hope to demonstrate that Schaeffer was not a presuppositionalist in the Van Til sense nor an evidentialist in the Warfield sense.
Instead I will argue that Schaeffer's approach was more like that of a verificationalist. However, in seeking to understand Schaeffer's apologetics, we do well to remember that he did not regard himself as an
academic apologist but as a front-line evangelist. Thus, rather than try
to squeeze his apologetics into the mold of any particular theoretical
methodology, we need to view him as a practitioner interested in reaching individuals with the truth of Jesus Christ. As Schaeffer himself
noted, he did not believe "there is any one apologetic which meets the
needs of all people."[2]

THE USE OF ASSUMPTIONS AND HIDDEN PREMISES

In his book *Francis Schaeffer's Apologetics: A Critique*, Thomas Morris criticizes Schaeffer for failing to undertake "careful formal analyses" and for not succeeding "in demonstrating the necessity of his position."[3] Far from regarding Schaeffer as a rationalist, Morris has argued that his strategy was that of a "pre-evangelistic, presuppositional apologetic." He believes that the main thrust of Schaeffer's scheme

> is carried through by a tripartite argument from design intended to communicate the inadequacies of antithetically non-Christian presuppositions and the truthfulness of basic Christian presuppositional claims.[4]

Although Schaeffer nowhere identifies his apologetic as an argument from design, Morris thinks that his focus on the non-Christian positions of atheism, irrationality, and amorality "correspond to three major areas of human philosophical enquiry traditionally known as metaphysics, epistemology and ethics, respectively."[5] These, he feels, are the three divisions or approaches of Schaeffer's argument from design.

By metaphysics, Schaeffer meant the question of Being and the existence of mankind. He agreed with Sartre that "the basic philosophic question is that something is there rather than nothing being there."[6] However, Morris detects a presupposition in Schaeffer's metaphysical argument with his rejection of an impersonal beginning to the universe. He argues that the three problems raised by Schaeffer about personality in an impersonal universe are not fully argued by him. The three problems are: (1) human aspirations for personal fulfillment in a universe that is finally impersonal are ultimately unfulfillable; (2) personality could never have arisen from the impersonal; and (3) an impersonal universe has a problem of unity and diversity, for it allows no special significance to any particular configuration. Furthermore, Morris suggests that all Schaeffer manages to establish "is that a personal beginning and ultimate ground of being is needed for a universe containing human personality. The question is still unanswered as to what specific kind of personality began, and is foundational to, the universe."[7] Thus one cannot adjudicate between rival positions such as Judaism, Islam, or polytheism, and Schaeffer has no grounds for his specific conclusions that orthodox Christian presuppositions are the answer, never mind his claim that they are the only ones that answer the problems facing man. Morris maintains that because "such conclusions are beyond the valid extensions of design argument, Schaeffer fails to complete the argument in its own valid form."[8] He also criticizes Schaeffer for not disclosing that the source of two specifications he makes—that God must be personal-infinite and Trinitarian—is biblical revelation. Morris believes that Schaeffer "has presented them as if they were tightly argued conclusions, universally acceptable."[9]

WEAKNESS OF ARGUMENT

If the impersonal beginning of the universe is the presupposition rejected by Schaeffer in his metaphysical argument, rejecting the presupposition of a closed system of cause and effect is for Morris the epistemological counterpart.[10] Schaeffer regarded epistemology (i.e., the theory of knowledge or "how we know that we know") as the central problem facing Christians in communicating their faith. Yet Morris feels that he does not adequately address it and again says that "the argument from design cannot lead directly from the data being considered to the specific orthodox Christian presuppositions being put forth by Schaeffer."[11] In particular, he suggests that in "proposing the Christian epistemological base to be propositional, verbalized revelation, Schaeffer does not argue its necessity but its possibility."[12] Morris accepts that Schaeffer's "direction of argumentation" has a "significant value" in showing Christianity to be "a reasonable philosophical position." However, he maintains that the argument presented by Schaeffer cannot adjudicate between Schaeffer's own system and other possible systems that also hold to the uniformity of natural causes in an open system.[13]

Morris speculates that Schaeffer recognized the limitation of his argument given the more gentle tone he adopted. For example, after pointing out the data to be considered and the problems to be solved, he presents his set of orthodox Christian presuppositions as a specific type of open system which, *if true*, would adequately explain the data and answer the problems.[14]

However, it is Morris's complaint that Schaeffer moves from "if Christianity is true" to "therefore, Christianity is true." The "logical gap between possibility and necessary actuality has, in his move, been jumped unwarrantedly as it was in the metaphysical argument."[15] Yet again, Schaeffer is regarded by Morris as seeking a solution by first "postulating biblical revelation" as the source of the Christian answers and then beginning to enumerate those answers.[16] Although Morris does not deal with it, it should be noted that Schaeffer's epistemological argument is also considered defective by some writers because of what they regard as his inaccuracies. His historical analysis and his understanding of secular and religious thinkers have been strongly criticized.[17] One scholar, Richard Pierard, has claimed that trying to fit different thinkers into his preconceived interpretation has led Schaeffer to be guilty of a "distortion of the past and outright myth-making." He regards these flaws to be so serious that they place Schaeffer's whole interpretative system in jeopardy.[18]

Meanwhile, returning to Morris, he finds Schaeffer's moral argument to be his weakest and declares that Schaeffer's conclusions are reached "after presenting only a group of generalized claims and arguments [which are] most highly disputable if not plainly false."[19] He criticizes Schaeffer's very basic assumption about the dilemma of man (who is capable of both great beauty and horrible cruelty) as "a loaded claim" and states that "this very first move would be unacceptable from various philosophical positions which consider such terms finally meaningless."[20] Morris believes that Schaeffer's claim to prove the moral necessity of the Christian presuppositions "would require an examination and demonstrated negative evaluation of all other possible basic presuppositions" and that this is an impossible task.[21] He also maintains that Schaeffer must substantiate his claim that men everywhere have the same basic underlying moral standard through anthropological data. Morris finds Schaeffer's arguments about a moral continuity or discontinuity to man to assume

> many notions having to do with his particular generic view of humanity (presumably arising from such orthodox doctrines as original sin), which he never articulates, and which function as hidden premises in the argument, rendering it unconvincing if not completely incomprehensible to those who do not already share the same notions.[22]

The Limits of Foundationalism

With his various "assumptions" and "hidden premises," one can see why Morris regarded Schaeffer as a presuppositionalist in his apologetics. While Morris does not mention Van Til by name, Forrest Baird claims that "Schaeffer was heavily influenced by Van Til," and Peter Hicks regards him as "one of Van Til's best-known followers."[23] As stated in the opening paragraph, I wish to show that Schaeffer was not a presuppositionalist in the Van Tilan sense, but first I want to consider the rationale behind the criticism of Schaeffer by Morris. As we saw in the previous chapter, Gordon Lewis has accused Morris of "making no serious attempt to expound Schaeffer's views with any degree of objectivity."[24] I would not go as far as Lewis, but I do think there is an unacknowledged element of subjectivity in Morris's writing. In criticizing Schaeffer for reaching conclusions "unwarranted by any argument offered" and presenting them with the "finality of a tightly reasoned conclusion," we need to remember that his objection is not to a rational approach. Rather, it is to the alleged lack of rational argument and evidence. In making such an objection, Morris reveals in his own approach a hidden assumption of evidentialism.

Evidentialism maintains that "a belief is rational for a person only if that person has sufficient evidence or arguments or reasons for that belief."[25] Evidentialism is rooted in classical foundationalism, which constructs knowledge "by first laying a very secure, undoubtable foundation and then building other truths on that base."[26] Beliefs that are part of a foundation—basic beliefs—must be self-evident or indis-

putable, and thus only a few very secure propositions are permitted in
the foundation. Although he does not refer to evidentialism by name,
Morris seems to go along with it in his criticism of Schaeffer for making moves in his argument without warrant—i.e., for lacking evidence
for some of his claims or conclusions. It is not really surprising to find
that Morris has absorbed evidentialism, given that classical foundationalism has been so pervasive in Western philosophy, including
among Christian thinkers. As David Clark has pointed out, just as "critics of Christian knowledge have assumed it in their attack, so advocates
have presupposed it in their defense."[27]

REFORMED EPISTEMOLOGY

However, in recent years Reformed epistemology, particularly through
the writings of Nicholas Wolterstorff and Alvin Plantinga, has launched
a serious challenge to evidentialism. By highlighting the narrow, restrictive foundation of knowledge in evidentialism, Reformed epistemology
has shown how that philosophy eliminates "many beliefs humans do
normally and correctly accept as knowledge."[28] As one Reformed critic
has written:

> [S]urely one is perfectly rational in believing that one had breakfast
> this morning, that there is an external world, and that one's wife is a
> person . . . classical foundationalism requires that they be supported
> by an argument from properly basic beliefs. But no one has ever pro-
> duced a good argument for these beliefs.[29]

Plantinga queries whether it is even rational to accept classical
foundationalism given that it is not a properly basic belief, nor can it
be inferred from one's basic beliefs. He concludes that it does not sat-
isfy its own first condition for rationality, and so he regards it as
bankrupt. For Plantinga, insofar "as the evidentialist objection is rooted
in classical foundationalism, it is poorly rooted indeed."[30]

Wolterstorff notes that evidentialism is "peculiarly modern," and
that until the modern age, "Christian apologetics consisted mainly not
in giving or defending arguments *for* Christianity, but rather in answer-

ing objections *to* Christianity."[31] Rather than seeking to prove the existence of God, Reformed epistemology holds that it is entirely rational to start with belief in God. Plantinga argues that belief in God resembles belief in other minds in that it is produced immediately without the support of other beliefs. Belief in God may be accepted as basic, and though you may not have proof or argument for such belief, you do not need them. Yet Plantinga maintains that a Christian's belief in God "can be perfectly rational even if he knows of no cogent argument, deductive or inductive, for the existence of God—indeed, even if there is no such argument."[32]

Nevertheless, Reformed epistemology does not regard belief in God as groundless or arbitrary. Plantinga distinguishes between *evidence* and *grounds*, the former being what apologists look for in theistic proofs, while the latter is more straightforward. Direct experience provides grounds to justify belief even without argumentation. One's experience of God appropriately grounds belief in His existence.[33] Reformed epistemologists stress the internal testimony of the Holy Spirit as confirming, for example, that the Bible is the reliable revelation from God. Stephen Evans believes that those who dismiss this Reformed approach as fideism (i.e., irrational faith based solely upon personal experience) try to understand it in evidentialist terms.[34] He says that it should be understood in externalist terms, which means

> that the factors that determine whether or not I am justified or warranted in holding my belief do not have to be internal to my consciousness. At bottom the externalist says that what properly "grounds" a belief is the relationship of the believer to reality.[35]

For Reformed epistemologists such as Evans, the biblical story is self-authenticating in the sense that "through the work of the Spirit the story itself produces a conviction of its truth in persons, and it is in that sense epistemologically basic."[36]

I would not wish to endorse all the claims that Reformed epistemology makes for itself, nor regard it as providing a complete explanation. Nevertheless, one can accept that it has mortally wounded the classical foundationalism of evidentialism. Thus one must question the validity of the evidentialist presupposition behind Morris's criticism of Schaeffer for lacking a warrant for the conclusions reached. Even if Schaeffer's arguments lack proof and validity for the claims made, the requirement for such proof and validity lacks warranty in itself. The criticism by Morris does not therefore invalidate Schaeffer's argumentation or his apologetics, which remain a helpful option for those engaging in discussion with non-Christians. Furthermore, it must be stated that even if evidentialism had not been discredited by Reformed epistemology, Morris would only be justified in his criticism of Schaeffer if the latter were adopting an evidentialist approach and could therefore be assessed in purely evidentialist terms. Yet it is Morris himself who points out the various "assumptions," "hidden premises," and "loaded claims" within Schaeffer's arguments. Clearly Schaeffer is not a strict evidentialist, for he is making use of presuppositions within his apologetical approach.

OLD PRINCETONIAN INFLUENCE

However, as stated in the opening paragraph of this chapter, I believe that Schaeffer was not a presuppositionalist in the Van Tilan sense of the word, nor an evidentialist like Warfield. To properly evaluate Schaeffer's apologetic approach, we need to understand his intellectual roots and his aim. Intellectually, he was influenced by both the scientific rationality of the Old Princeton theology and the presuppositionalism of Van Til and Kuyper's Dutch school. In addition to the above two streams of theological thought flowing into Schaeffer's mind, there was also a strong undercurrent of pietistic spirituality influencing Schaeffer's ministry.

Turning first to the Princetonian influence, as mentioned in Chapter One, Schaeffer studied under Gresham Machen at Westminster Theological Seminary and absorbed his enthusiasm for the Old Princeton theology. Machen believed "that science, philosophy, and religion all dealt with the same thing—facts."[37] He was concerned that the chief tendency in modern thought was away from direct knowledge of facts to subjective experience. Machen rejected the new view that the historic creeds of the Christian faith are only "the changing expression of a unitary Christian experience." For him, the creeds were a "setting forth of those facts upon which experience is based." He believed that Christianity, like any other historical phenomenon, "must be investigated on the basis of historical evidence."[38] Oliver Buswell, editor of *The Bible Today*, for which Schaeffer wrote in the 1940s, was another source of Princetonian influence on Schaeffer. As Lewis points out, Buswell was an inductive apologist who maintained that human reason is "responsible for critically testing truth claims by the observable evidence and casual inference."[39]

Both Machen and Buswell reflected the nineteenth-century Princeton tradition of "the Baconian ideal which held that the duty of science was first to observe and register the facts and then to generalise about them."[40] They, like the Old Princetonians, held that the work of the theologian was like that of the scientist. The strong emphasis on discovering facts and the role played by reason in this has led some evangelical writers to suggest that the Princeton approach was "overly sanguine about the powers of rational apologetics."[41] As detailed in Chapter One, the Old Princeton theology was influenced by Scottish Common Sense philosophy. This has led George Marsden to observe that while "Calvinists had maintained that the human mind was blinded in mankind's Fall from innocence, in the Common Sense version, the intellect seemed to suffer from a slight astigmatism only."[42]

THE VAN TILAN INFLUENCE

In sharp contrast to the Old Princeton theology, the approach of Abraham Kuyper (1837–1920) and his Dutch school held that individuals, including their rational capacities, needed to be redeemed before they could reason properly. Far from attempting to argue someone toward a knowledge of God, Kuyper insisted that "knowledge of God is founded, not upon something prior to itself, but rather on God himself breathing into the minds of humans."[43] Cornelius Van Til, under whom Schaeffer studied at Westminster for two years, used Kuyper's notion of the antithesis (i.e., that an absolute antithesis exists in all of life between the believer and unbeliever) to develop his pre-suppositional apologetics.

Although Van Til accepted a point of contact with the non-Christian, he did not believe there is any neutral, common epistemological foundation between a Christian and a non-Christian. To Van Til, all "empirical observation is inescapably theory-laden (there are no uninterpreted 'brute facts') . . . and unbelievers (like believers) are not all unbiased, impartial or without motive or good."[44] If a person does not intellectually acknowledge his or her need to presuppose God, any attempt to reason and interpret experience is not intelligible. John Frame has noted that for Van Til, presuppositionalism did not denote apriorism, but the "pre- in presupposition refers to the 'pre-eminence' of the presupposition with respect to our other beliefs."[45] Like Kuyper, who viewed knowledge in terms of the overall relationships it involves, Van Til recognized a unity in knowledge, and he argued that "the very essence of knowledge is to bring our thoughts into agreement with God's revealed Word."[46] For Van Til, thinking God's thought after Him was to be the rule in every sphere of life, including apologetics.

The evidentialist apologetics of those influenced by the Old Princetonian approach and the presuppositionalism of Van Til provided Schaeffer with a rich intellectual heritage. In his own apologetics there are elements of both traditions, and this has led to criticism by Clark Pinnock that Schaeffer "floats back and forth between these two very different standpoints as suits him."[47] Was Schaeffer inconsistent, or was he simply eclectic in his approach, or was he attempting to do something new?

HOW SCHAEFFER UNDERSTOOD *PRESUPPOSITIONS*

Schaeffer freely used the word *presuppositions* and was convinced about "the importance of thinking in terms of presuppositions, especially concerning truth."[48] As mentioned earlier, many writers, including Thomas Morris and Peter Hicks, therefore tend to view Schaeffer, albeit incorrectly, as a presuppositionalist in his apologetics. It is true that, like Van Til, Schaeffer believed there "are no neutral facts, for facts are God's facts" and maintained that "there is no use talking today until the presuppositions are taken into account."[49] Furthermore, Schaeffer felt there was a "weakness" in the Princetonian apologetics because of its "assuming that the man has the same presuppositions as you have."[50] Indeed he even argued that the "floodwaters of secular thought and liberal theology overwhelmed the Church because the leaders did not understand the importance of combating a false set of presuppositions."[51] However, and this is a crucial difference from Van Til, Schaeffer did not believe that you have to require the non-Christian to presuppose God before you can have a meaningful discussion with him.

While there were no neutral facts, Schaeffer believed there was common ground between the Christian and non-Christian because

> in reality no one can live logically according to his own non-Christian presuppositions, and consequently, because he is faced with the real world and himself, in practice you will find a place where you can talk.[52]

In his book *The God Who Is There*, Schaeffer did not criticize Van Til by name, but in a lecture he gave in 1963 he referred to their different approaches.[53] Speaking to a small group at L'Abri, Schaeffer said there was "a weakness" and "a mistake" in Van Til's argument "in saying that you can't even talk to a man until he accepts your presuppositions."[54]

Van Til's view reduced apologetics to the defense of the faith and giving an explanation to the Christian, and Schaeffer lamented that "at the point where they could reach others, they [the Van Tilans] just stop." Although he was "very unhappy to say it," Schaeffer stated that "in practice, in some ways, Van Til sounds almost the same as Barth. In both cases there is no real discussion."[55] Such an interpretation of Van Til, and especially the comparison of him with Barth, is strongly contested by Van Tilan scholars. For example, William Edgar, the present Professor of Apologetics at Westminster Theological Seminary, regards the suggestion that Van Til accepted no common ground as a significant error. In contrast to Barth, who resisted any natural knowledge of God, Van Til assigned "the point of contact to human consciousness, which is constantly aware of God."[56] Van Til believed his approach drew upon Romans 1 and was consistent with Calvin's idea of the sense of deity.

Thus Van Tilans reject Schaeffer's criticism that Van Til was, in practice, no different from Barth. Yet it must be said that Schaeffer genuinely believed that Van Til's apologetics prevented meaningful discussion. For Schaeffer, drawing upon the Old Princetonian approach, apologetics was to be used for evangelism by "the communication of the gospel to the present generation in terms they can understand."[57] He sought to do that by pushing the non-Christians to the logical (but unacceptable) conclusion of their own presuppositions and then presenting a rational argument in favor of the Christian truth-claims, which do not contradict reality.

Underlying Core Belief

So what about presuppositions? What status did Schaeffer afford them? How exactly did he think they operated? He defined a presupposition as a belief that "consciously or unconsciously affects the way a person subsequently reasons."[58] Presuppositions are the most basic tenets of a person's belief system. Because they affect how a person thinks about truth, and since there has been a change in how people come to truth, Schaeffer believed that now, "more than ever before, a presuppositional apologetic is imperative."[59] Yet his understanding of presupposition was quite different from Van Til's. For the latter, the term indicated the role that divine revelation ought to play in human thought. Van Til used *presupposition* transcendentally, that is, as the ground or framework that gives each person meaning. A presupposition was the precondition whereby things have meaning and value.[60] By contrast, Schaeffer understood presuppositions to be the underlying core personal beliefs of each individual. It was by drawing out these basic beliefs that Schaeffer managed to find a point of contact with an individual and so engage in meaningful dialogue. Thus for Schaeffer, presuppositions were an apologetical tool to be used to open people up to the truth-claims of Christianity—to challenge the basis of their existing beliefs, and to commend the reasonableness of Christian belief. Convinced that Christian presuppositions match the real experience of life, he urged people to consider the different sets of presuppositions and decide "which of these fits the facts of what is."[61]

One long-term worker at L'Abri, Barry Seagren, spent some time studying under Van Til at Westminster Theological Seminary and came to realize that Van Til and Schaeffer meant different things by the word *presuppositions*. He believed that for Van Til they were axioms—i.e., starting points that couldn't be questioned. Meanwhile, for Schaeffer they were only basic ideas that he used as part of his strenuous efforts to reach non-believers with Christian arguments. In his 1963 key lecture on apologetics, Schaeffer had criticized Van Til for failing to engage in meaningful argument with non-Christians unless they presupposed God. However, when Jerram Barrs first visited L'Abri in 1967, Schaeffer was still encouraging students to read Van Til so as to "draw upon his insights about the importance of presuppositions."[62] Yet as Barrs noted, in contrast to Van Til, Schaeffer was using presuppositions as an argument for the existence of God. Indeed Seagren suggests that Schaeffer should really be seen as an evidentialist but "an evidentialist of ideas." While others bring in archaeology or the historical evidence for the resurrection, Schaeffer did not. Instead "he presented ideas: the personal God, man made in His image, the Fall etc and asked 'does this explain the world we live in?'"[63]

CRITICISM FROM VAN TIL

It wasn't only Schaeffer's close colleagues such as Seagren and Barrs who realized that he afforded presuppositions a different status and role than Van Til. Van Til himself was quick to spot the different approach and was eager "to distance himself and the presuppositional school of thought from Schaeffer's apologetic method."[64] In an academic paper that became a part of his apologetics curriculum at Westminster, Van Til strongly criticized Schaeffer for the way he handled presuppositions. Although it was very easy to gain the impression from Schaeffer's terminology that he was a presuppositionalist, Van Til complained that

at the critical moment Schaeffer seeks to show the unbeliever that Christianity is true because it is in accord with fact, and in accord with logic as the non-Christian understands fact and logic. At no time does Schaeffer point out the fact that on the presupposition of the unbeliever the words "fact" and "logic" have no meaning. In particular, Schaeffer over and over again appeals to "reason" as though it were something on the nature of which Christians and non-Christians agree. In short Schaeffer's approach in apologetics is not basically different from that of the late Edward Carnell.[65]

By inviting the non-Christian to choose between Christian and non-Christian presuppositions on the basis of which of them best "fits the facts of what is," Van Til believed that Schaeffer treated presuppositions as though they were hypotheses. He criticized Schaeffer for allowing the non-Christian to judge whether Christianity best met the facts of the world around him. Van Til was convinced that although Schaeffer kept saying Christianity is the only answer, he "also keeps saying that Christianity must prove itself true to apostate man in terms of the standard that this apostate man has devised."[66] Thus Van Til argued that for all practical purposes, Schaeffer still employed the traditional method of apologetics. When Van Til first read a copy of the lectures that Schaeffer delivered in 1965 at Wheaton College, he expected to find "in them a frank assertion to the effect that we can find no effective point of contact with the modern unbeliever except in terms of the self-identifying Christ of Scripture."[67] He expressed his considerable disappointment that Schaeffer failed to make such an assertion and instead proposed to engage in conversation that was designed to allow the non-Christian to "discover the truth of the Biblical system for himself."[68]

Van Til believed that Schaeffer had not taken "sufficient account of the blinded condition of the sinner who can only misconstrue the very possibility of the truth of Scripture."[69] He recognized that in Schaeffer's writings, the great sin of modern thought is its irrationalism. While commending Schaeffer for seeking to counteract the irrationalism of neo-orthodox thinking, Van Til maintained that "it is just as necessary to counteract the rationalism of the classical view of truth."[70] Van Til rebukes Schaeffer for "consistently thinking in terms of Christianity as something additional to naturalism." He suggests that Schaeffer's approach is more like that which you would expect to hear from a Roman Catholic theologian or philosopher.[71] Van Til acknowledged that he was a sinner until "God reached down to change my inmost disposition. . . . Only now that I live do I understand something of the nature of the death from which I have been rescued."[72] Thus for Van Til no one could enter into a right relationship with God "unless by the regenerating and enlightening work of the Holy Spirit, we believe the words that he has spoken of himself in Scripture."[73] Without presupposing this truth, apologetics is useless.

Schaeffer and Van Til both used the term *presuppositions*, but clearly each gave it a different meaning. Far from wanting students at Westminster to think that Schaeffer's approach to apologetics was essentially the same as his own, Van Til compared Schaeffer to Edward Carnell. Like Carnell, Schaeffer expresses a commitment to the idea that we must presuppose God's revelation to man in Christ through the Scriptures as absolutely authoritative but then permits man's rationality to decide whether Christianity is true or not. As mentioned earlier, for Van Til this meant treating Christian presuppositions as though they were hypotheses.[74] Schaeffer's willingness, on the basis of John 17:21, to treat love between Christians as the "final apologetic" was also criticized by Van Til. Comparing him to Carnell who set up the non-believer as judge with respect to the truth-claims of believers, Van Til accused Schaeffer of setting up "the same apostate man as judge over the spiritual claims of believers."[75]

CHALLENGED BY VAN TIL

Concerned over Schaeffer's approach to apologetics and the confusion created by his use of the word *presuppositions*, Van Til challenged him through a series of personal letters. As Burson and Walls point out, instead of clarifying his position Schaeffer simply refused to respond. There appeared to be three reasons for this attitude. First, as an evangelist he was consumed with the day-to-day conversion of souls and could not justify the energy it would take to engage in an academic debate. Second, he continued to respect Van Til and believed he was drawing upon a great deal of his thinking. And, third, knowing how ugly academic debates could become, especially those involving Van Til, Schaeffer wanted to avoid heated exchanges.[76]

However, it is fascinating to note that in the later editions of *The God Who Is There*, Schaeffer deleted the reference in Chapter One to the necessity of presuppositional apologetics. In the early editions of the book he wrote, "Man thinks differently concerning truth, and *so now for us, more than ever before, a presuppositional apologetic is imperative.*"[77] Yet, by 1982 when *The Complete Works of Francis Schaeffer* were published, he cut out everything after the word *truth*. Given that the sentence originally appeared in italics so as to underline its importance, its removal from the later editions was clearly a deliberate choice by Schaeffer. One can only speculate the reason, but it does seem fair to suggest that Schaeffer realized the confusion being caused by referring to a presuppositional apologetic. He continued to talk about presuppositions, but the status he afforded presuppositions continued to be quite different from that of Van Til's presuppositional apologetic. While presuppositions—in the sense of a person's underlying core beliefs—played a key part in Schaeffer's apologetics, he was *not* a presuppositional apologist. It is quite misleading, therefore, for Peter Hicks to describe Schaeffer as "one of Van Til's best-known followers."[78]

THE USE OF PRESUPPOSITIONS AS HYPOTHESES

Gordon Lewis suggests, given Schaeffer's view that presuppositions can be verified and shown to be true or false, that he "would communicate better if he called presuppositions 'hypotheses.'"[79] Indeed when Schaeffer was first published in 1968, Colin Brown was quick to notice that his approach could be compared with a set of hypotheses in science. As with a good hypothesis, Schaeffer in his argument attempted to "make sense of the observed facts and take into account the maximum number of other observed facts."[80] Brown noted that Schaeffer did not attempt to prove God's existence but took it for granted. In presenting the belief system of the Bible, Schaeffer argued that it made good sense of "what is." For Brown, this is like a hypothesis that presents in the first instance "an unproved theory designed to account for something hitherto not understood."[81] Lewis is critical—and deservedly so—of Thomas Morris for describing Schaeffer's approach as presuppositionalist even though he (i.e., Morris) is aware of the way in which Schaeffer treats presuppositions like hypotheses. Twice Morris "quotes Schaeffer to the effect that he is testing presuppositions (obviously as hypotheses rather than untestable presuppositions) by whether or not they fit the facts."[82]

Despite using the word "presupposition," it is clear that Schaeffer's starting point was more like a hypothesis. And it is important that we grasp that Schaeffer is not an "inconsistent presuppositionalist," as Kenneth Harper suggests in *Bibliotheca Sacra*. Nor is his approach to apologetics just a "milder form of presuppositionalism" as David Clark would have us understand.[83] Schaeffer's use of hypotheses places him outside presuppositionalism, for certainly presuppositionalism rejects any notion of neutral facts or common ground. Yet I am indebted to Jock McGregor for the insight that if the concept of antithesis is regarded as the heart of presuppositionalism, then Schaeffer can still be seen as a presuppositionalist. Indeed, given the emphasis Schaeffer gave to antithesis, I believe his approach could be understood as very presuppositional. However, when we consider the overall picture, I think Gordon Lewis is correct to identify Schaeffer's approach as owing much to the verificational method of apologetics.

The verificational method starts with tentative hypotheses from any type of experience and then "subjects these hypotheses to testing and confirmation or disconfirmation by the coherence of their account with the relevant lines of data."[84] The verificational method is sometimes considered a type of evidential apologetics because it has an inductive element whereby it tests hypotheses by their conformity with the empirical data. However, it is also sometimes seen as a form of presuppositionalism given its deductive element that starts from assumed premises. Lewis argues that the verificational method is neither a form of evidential or presuppositional apologetics but is a third method, having a distinctly different, logical starting point—i.e., a hypothesis to be tested. Lewis suggests that the verificational method in apologetics has existed explicitly since Elton Trueblood's *The Knowledge of God* was published in 1939. Yet the scholar most closely identified with the verificational method was Edward Carnell.[85]

EDWARD CARNELL

In 1948 Carnell published his prize-winning volume, *An Introduction to Christian Apologetics*. He recognized that the basic doctrines of historic biblical Christianity appeared to the modern mind "to be but figments of superstition and imagination, gratuitously assumed by timorous supernaturalists."[86] And that was a view that Carnell, with all his intellectual brilliance, sought to challenge. He believed that the reason of man, corrupted by nature through sin, although darkened, was "not extinguished." Thus it had important interpretative functions. In setting tests so that a person might recognize truth, Carnell argued that a judgment could be said to be true and could be trusted "when it sticks together with all the facts of our experience."[87] Thus there had to be consistency, and this consistency had to be systematic. By consistency he meant obedience to the law of contradiction, for where you find contradiction, you "can be sure that truth is conspicuous by its absence."[88] Carnell maintained that this law (also called the law of non-contradiction) was innate to each person, for "if we have not innate knowledge of the rules for right thinking, right thinking cannot start."[89]

Carnell pointed out that he was not attempting to demonstrate God's existence by rational argument. Instead he was merely attempting to explain data "which makes the hypothesis of God's existence coherent."[90] Recognizing that not all people were troubled with rational objections to the faith, he acknowledged that he was one of those whose "heart cannot believe what my mind rejects as false."[91] Yet Carnell also recognized the limits of rationality and noted that natural reason was incompetent and incapable of working out a complete view of God or a philosophy of life "without a special revelation from God."[92] Unlike earlier Christian apologists who adopted a firmly evidentialist approach and who argued to an objective conclusion on the basis of "simple facts," Carnell acknowledged the myth of neutrality. He believed that it was useless to say, "just stay with the facts," as each person makes assumptions in his or her thinking. Everyone makes "assumptions because we must make assumptions to think at all. All knowledge is inferential and all inferences are assumptions. Knowledge is the mind's construction of *meaning*, and properly construed meaning is truth."[93]

Carnell believed that people make numerous assumptions in everyday life when dealing with simple facts like broken glass, dead batteries, or the smell of gas. Each fact-situation has to be explained, and your explanation is in fact a hypothesis. When there is a number of possible explanations, that "one which leads us coherently into all of our experience is the true one."[94] Long before the ground-breaking work of scholars such as Michael Polanyi and Thomas Kuhn made it fashionable to query the notion of pure empiricism and complete objectivity, Carnell was doing just that. In rejecting the claims of science to deal only with absolute facts, Carnell argued that the procedures employed by the scientists were really no different from the ordinary person making everyday assumptions. The only difference he allowed scientists was that they conducted their procedures on a more refined scale. Carnell challenged the worldview assumptions that the scientist must presuppose and complained

> that the scientist rejects the Christian world-view because it involves certain nonempirical, metaphysical hypotheses, while assuming for himself a truckload, each of which goes as much beyond sensory observation as does the Christian's postulate of the God Who has revealed Himself in Scripture.[95]

PROBABİLİTY OF PROOF

Carnell accepted that proof for the Christian faith—as with any worldview—could not rise above rational probability. For him, Christianity was a way of life, and because it was not an "unabridged edition of the Pythagorean theorem, it cannot enjoy the demonstrable certainty of the latter." However, he maintained that the more the evidence increases for a given hypothesis, the more the strength of probability increases. Carnell realized that some Christians would be disappointed by his admission of probability in Christianity. Yet he suggested that this was actually a strength because if his approach was correct, "then the system of Christianity can be refuted only by probability."[96] Convinced that neutrality in metaphysics is impossible, Carnell believed that at this level (i.e., the level of ultimate meaning), "the system of Christianity and the system of non-Christianity have absolutely no truth in common."[97] However, unlike Cornelius Van Til, Carnell argued that as long as ultimates are not talked about, the Christian and the non-Christian can enjoy common ground. Because of common grace, the non-Christian is not consistent in his worldview in that "he uses Christian presuppositions to give frame and support to his pagan ultimates."[98] Thus for practical purposes, Carnell argued that there was a genuine common ground between the Christian and the inconsistent non-Christian.

Carnell saw the purpose of Christian apologetics as removing from critics any excuse for not repenting before God. He was convinced that "men who refuse Christ because of presumed 'logical errors' in Christianity are men with a self-righteousness in the area of knowledge. They are resting on props which must be pulled away."[99] Nevertheless, he recognized that you cannot argue a person into becoming a Christian, and he believed that the apologist was to "gently refute error, then preach the gospel, for men are saved by the power of the gospel." Indeed he stressed that the "power of repentance comes from the effective agency of the Holy Spirit, and apart from this power, no man can know Christ's saving grace."[100]

CARNELL AND THE VERIFICATIONAL INFLUENCE

The similarity in the way Schaeffer used presuppositions and the role of hypotheses in Carnell's apologetics is clear. In fact, on the basis of their similarity, Gordon Lewis makes a strong case for regarding Schaeffer as a verificationalist both in terms of his use of explicitly verificational terminology and his methodology.[101] However, it must be said that at times Lewis is a little too keen to claim Schaeffer as a verificationalist. While accepting a similarity between Schaeffer and Carnell in their willingness to test the reasonableness of their hypotheses, I question the wisdom of placing Schaeffer totally in the verificationalist school of apologetics. For example, Schaeffer would not have shared Carnell's appreciation of Søren Kierkegaard's emphasis on inward experience. Although Carnell did not uncritically endorse existentialism and did not accept the claim that there is a polarity tension between objective certainty and subjective faith, he was very willing to acknowledge his indebtedness to Kierkegaard.[102]

Nevertheless, Schaeffer's approach to apologetics is more like that of a verificationalist such as the early Carnell than an evidentialist like Warfield or a presuppositionalist like Van Til. In a journal article published in 1973, E. R. Geehan compared Schaeffer's testing of Christian presuppositions concerning the world and mankind to Carnell's approach and noted their similarity.[103] In this, Geehan, who himself adopts a presuppositionalist approach to apologetics, was following the criticism of Schaeffer made by Van Til in the 1960s when he compared him with Carnell. While finding aspects of Carnell's first apologetic book—published in 1948—to be helpful, Van Til argued that "gradually, however, in his later works his method became more and more like that of Aquinas and Butler."[104] Van Til told his students at Westminster that "for all of Schaeffer's claim to use a presuppositional or biblical approach, his method is still basically similar to that of the traditional Aquinas-Butler approach."[105] Given that Schaeffer regarded Thomas Aquinas as being responsible for opening the intellect to much that was destructive, he would have found the comparison with him very damning. While he did not engage in a public dispute with Van Til, it does appear that Schaeffer did attempt to distance himself from Carnell.

Schaeffer did not acknowledge in his books any influence on his apologetics by Carnell. However, in his 1948 article on apologetics, he did refer to Carnell's book.[106] It may be that Schaeffer's later failure to mention Carnell, thus distancing himself, arose from a desire to avoid coming under heavy fire by Van Til. In 1964 Van Til wrote *The Case for Calvinism* in which he sought to demolish three other authors, one being Edward Carnell. Among many criticisms, Van Til claimed that the tests of truth employed by Carnell "are identical to those used by unbelieving philosophy, especially Kantian philosophy."[107] As mentioned earlier, Schaeffer was anxious to avoid a public dispute with Van Til.

Part of the reason for this was his conviction, deeply held since his spiritual crisis of 1951, that personal attacks were "completely ruinous spiritually" to those who employed them. The other possible reason why Schaeffer wanted to distance himself from Carnell was the fact that the latter had come to be viewed with suspicion by many evangelicals because of his apparent difficulties with the historical reliability of the biblical revelation.[108] Given Schaeffer's strong commitment to the inerrancy of Holy Scripture, identifying with Carnell was in itself just undesirable.

SCHAEFFER'S DIFFERENT STYLE

Perhaps a more fundamental reason why Schaeffer maintained a distance from Carnell was the simple fact that there was a distance between them. True, Schaeffer drew upon Carnell's approach to apologetics in relation to making one's presuppositions open to verification. However, in relation to other aspects—for example, the question of probability of proof—Schaeffer drew more upon the evidentialists than from Carnell. Schaeffer was not committed to Carnell's method in the same way that he was not committed to any particular theoretical methodology. Schaeffer, as stated at the beginning of this chapter, was a practitioner, not a theoretician, and in his own approach to apologetics he drew happily upon several different sources. In blending the evidentialist method of Warfield with the presuppositionalist method of Van Til, Schaeffer was adopting a similar approach to the verificational method of Carnell, which was in itself an integrationist approach. Indeed Carnell had written that since "apologetics is an art and not a science, there is no 'official' way to go about defending the Christian faith."[109]

However, it is wrong to depict Schaeffer as someone who was privately greatly influenced by Carnell but who publicly kept his distance out of fear. While Schaeffer was acquainted with Carnell's 1948 prize-winning book on apologetics, there is no indication from Schaeffer's private papers, discussions at L'Abri, or comments to close colleagues that he continued to follow Carnell. Indeed I am convinced that Schaeffer was following no one Christian scholar in particular but was forging a new style in apologetics to enable him to reach disillusioned or unchurched people. Schaeffer was first and foremost an evangelist with a burden in his heart to win people for Christ. Yet he believed that "my talking about metaphysics, morals and epistemology to certain individuals is a part of my evangelism just as much as when I get to the moment to show them that they are morally guilty and tell them that Christ died for them on the cross."[110] For Schaeffer, speaking and writing in the 1960s, not the sexual revolution but epistemology was "the central problem of our generation" because "the modern generation looks at knowledge in a way radically different from previous ones."[111]

Because positivism (which repudiated the possibility of a theological or metaphysical explanation of reality) had failed, all that was left for secular society was "cynicism or some mystical leap to knowing."[112] Schaeffer noted: "[W]e find a uniform need for an irrational experience to make some sense of life. Their views have brought them to a wall, and by an unrelated leap of faith they hope to clear the wall."[113] Given his conviction, as already mentioned in the previous chapter, that "rationality is needed to open the door to a vital relationship to God,"[114] Schaeffer made it a key battle of his apologetics to fight the loss of rationality. Thus his whole approach appears more evidentialist than does that of those who give a greater emphasis to the internal testimony of the Holy Spirit. Yet, unlike Warfield who endorsed the theistic proofs, Schaeffer felt that "all the classic proofs were worthless."[115]

RATIONALITY AND PERSONALITY

Indeed it is very important to grasp that although Schaeffer wanted to convince people that "there are good and sufficient reasons to know why Christianity is true,"[116] he was not an evidentialist in the traditional sense. For example, he did not focus on the integrity and reliability of the New Testament documents. Nor did he seek to develop a substantive historical case for the resurrection of Jesus Christ. Although Schaeffer appealed to "the universe and its form" as part of his total case, Burson and Walls find it striking that he never gave serious attention to classical cosmological and teleological arguments.[117] Instead Schaeffer, focusing on the "mannishness of man," gave importance to the question of personality and human significance. Just as he made the fight for rationality a key element in his apologetics because of the prevailing irrationalism in contemporary secular thought, so he stressed human personality against dominant impersonal worldviews. Schaeffer's emphasis on the "mannishness of man" in his apologetic undermined "the presuppositions of the dominant impersonal worldviews, while simultaneously providing a rational basis for hope, the two things Schaeffer thought most necessary to combat the naturalistic conditioning of the human race."[118]

At Schaeffer's particular moment of history, the great battle in Christian apologetics was against irrationalism and an impersonal worldview. The importance he attached to the role of rational argument in his apologetics and the priority he gave to the question of human personality reveals how keen Schaeffer was to challenge the spirit of the age. In Chapter Three it was noted that some of Schaeffer's L'Abri colleagues thought he was adopting the perspectability approach. By this they meant that at certain points, certain perspectives need to be emphasized, albeit they are not given a higher importance. I agree with this analysis of Schaeffer, and I believe that it applies not only to the style but also to the content of his apologetics. It helps explain why Schaeffer, without being a rationalist, gave rationality such importance and why his arguments were so different from the normal evidentialist approach.

AN ACADEMIC, AN APOLOGIST, OR AN EVANGELIST?

Again, it is impossible to understand Schaeffer, never mind properly evaluate his apologetics, unless we grasp that he was a practitioner and not a theoretician, and so interpret him in the context of what he sought to do. Much effort has been spent, most of it wasted, by academics attempting to shoehorn Schaeffer into some particular philosophical or apologetical methodology. Furthermore, I doubt whether it is profitable for scholars to dissect Schaeffer's writings as if they formed a carefully crafted—and much revised—philosophical or theological treatise. Schaeffer's books mainly emerged from his lectures and discussions at L'Abri, and as Colin Brown has rightly observed of one book, it must be read and judged for what it is: a "suggestive and provocative essay."[119] Schaeffer himself never tired of saying to visitors at L'Abri, "I'm not a philosopher but an evangelist." And as James Sire has said of him, "You have to take him on his own terms."[120]

However, Clark Pinnock is one who has refused to do that and has instead made a blistering attack on Schaeffer. He criticizes Schaeffer's "lack of credible scholarship," his "fuzzy and blurred presentations," and his "pseudohistorical" approach.[121] Pinnock has acknowledged that he wished "we could say that Schaeffer was just an evangelist and ward off his criticism, but his own claims and those made for him in the books and on film would not allow it."[122] It is certainly true that extravagant claims have been made for Schaeffer by his publishers, and this is most clearly seen in relation to his two film series. In promotional material for *Whatever Happened to the Human Race?* it was claimed that Schaeffer was "one of the world's most respected thinkers."[123] He was not, never claimed to be, and most surely must have been quite embarrassed by such claims. As James Packer has noted, "Schaeffer has been criticized as a grandiose guru, but the criticism is inept. It assumes a degree of egoism and calculation that was simply not there."[124]

So why did he tolerate others making such claims about him? First, as anyone who has been involved in commercial publishing will be aware, the author has very little influence over what the publishers say about him or her. Eager to market their products, most companies "talk up" their authors. But in Schaeffer's case, the second significant reason why he had to go along with the grandiose claims was the role of his son, Franky. It was he who produced the films and who was responsible for some of the more extravagant claims about his father. It is probably fair to say that Franky never fully grasped what his father's ministry was about in terms of the founding principle that they would allow the work to develop as the Lord led, that they would pray and wait upon the Lord, and that they would not solicit funds.[125] In moving, without further reflection, to plan the two film series and seeking to raise the necessary funds for the projects, Franky rode roughshod over this central principle of L'Abri.[126] Franky's style and claims about his father not only left Francis Schaeffer open to criticism but also caused problems within L'Abri.[127] Obviously Schaeffer's love for his son put blinders on his judgment, but some aspects of Franky's later behavior suggests that parental indulgence didn't do him any good either.[128]

WEAKNESS OF SCHOLARSHIP

However, Clark Pinnock is unwilling to acknowledge that the exaggerated claims about Schaeffer were only made by others and so views him as partly responsible. In therefore considering Schaeffer against the criteria of a great scholar, he finds him sadly lacking. Indeed he finds "large gaps" in Schaeffer's knowledge of the great thinkers and regards his writings as "pseudohistorical."[129] For Pinnock, Schaeffer's historical sweep of Western thought can simply be regarded as "pretentious."[130] Pinnock's criticism of Schaeffer is unfortunate because it is fundamentally unfair. The point made earlier by James Sire is very valid: you must take Schaeffer on his own terms—that is, view him as an evangelist. Schaeffer repeatedly stated that his interest was not in academic apologetics but in evangelism.[131] Given that Pinnock studied (and even worked) at L'Abri in the 1960s and knew of Schaeffer's passion for evangelism from firsthand experience, there is really no justification for his failing to view Schaeffer as an evangelist.

Of course, there are aspects of Schaeffer's work where his presentation may be fuzzy or blurred and points may be suggested rather than proved. But then, as Colin Brown points out, "many seminal works in the history of thought have done the same."[132] Furthermore, Schaeffer was not writing specifically to a scholarly crowd but was making a broad appeal to ordinary persons. As Burson and Walls note, Schaeffer, in common with C. S. Lewis, rejected the notion "that weighty metaphysical matters are the exclusive property of trained philosophers" and sought to communicate in "language and imagery that would be more readily accessible to the common person."[133] That Schaeffer helped free the philosophy of ideas from an academic elite and made it available to rank-and-file Christians as an apologetic tool is to be welcomed. Nor did he claim that his books contained the final word on any subject but merely that they put the issue on the table for discussion.

In an appendix to *The God Who Is There*, Schaeffer stated that while he was not a professional academic philosopher, the "more academically oriented philosopher" could deal with "more of the necessary details" that he had just alluded to. Yet, as you would expect from an evangelist, he was adamant that "all the cultural, intellectual or philosophic material is not to be separated from leading people to Christ."[134] People—not academia—was, and always remained, Schaeffer's over-riding concern.

TAKING TIME TO LOVE

His love of people, and in particular his desire to see people rescued by Christ, explains why Schaeffer gave so sacrificially of his time to individual people. He was convinced of the biblical truth that to enjoy the loving acceptance of God, "there must have been a moment in the past when by grace we accepted Christ as our Saviour and were therefore declared justified by God."[135] Schaeffer saw his mission, indeed his calling, as an evangelist, but an evangelist who dealt with the philosophical and intellectual questions that obscured the gospel.[136] Doing so meant treating all persons as individuals, given that they had a particular life story, personal intellectual misunderstandings, and perceptions distinctive to themselves. However, this was very time-consuming, emotionally draining, and pastorally demanding. Yet Schaeffer always sought to make the effort. Even when he was seriously ill with cancer and undergoing treatment in the USA, he continued to find time to talk with individuals and to conduct discussion groups.[137]

Schaeffer made the effort with individuals because he believed it was necessary (from an evangelistic perspective) and because he regarded each individual as worthy of the effort. Given that non-Christians do not live a life consistent with their own value-system and thus have a point of tension between their belief and reality, Schaeffer argued that

> the first consideration in our apologetics for modern man, whether factory-hand or research student, is to find the place where his tension exists. We will not always find it easy to do this. Many people

have never analyzed their own point of tension. Since the Fall man is separated from himself. Man is complicated, and he tries to bury himself in himself. Therefore, it will take time and it will cost something to discover what the person we are speaking to often has not yet discovered for himself.[138]

As Schaeffer noted, this sort of one-to-one ministry is not easy. It takes time, and it costs in terms of emotional energy, personal inconvenience, and spiritual struggle. Yet Francis and Edith Schaeffer gave unstintingly of themselves to countless individuals over the years. As one long-term worker observed of Schaeffer, "he was very good pastorally, very warm. He would take time, he listened and he treated people individually."[139]

Schaeffer gave of himself so that people could be brought into a personal relationship with Jesus Christ. To reach those beyond the church, who could not grasp the truth of the gospel, he was willing to work on a one-to-one basis. However, as stated above he did so not just from necessity but because the individual was worthy. Schaeffer warned that

to be engaged in personal "witness" as a duty or because our Christian circle exerts a social pressure on us, is to miss the whole point. The reason we do it is that the person before us is an image-bearer of God and he is an individual who is unique in the world.[140]

Love for individuals led Schaeffer to be willing to open his home to strangers, to warmly receive unexpected guests, and to spend hours with the spiritually lost. One Italian student who was a frequent visitor to L'Abri said of Francis and Edith Schaeffer that they "were willing to carry the burdens that all these multitude of people came with. Their life was busy indeed—meals to prepare, endless dishes to be made, mountains of washing—and picking up the pieces of broken lives."[141]

No doubt he didn't spend the same amount of time reading the original works of the great thinkers as did some evangelical academics. But then, unlike critics such as Clark Pinnock or Richard Pierard who complained about his lack of reading, Schaeffer wasn't cocooned in a college. Schaeffer did not choose the leisurely life of academic reflection seated safely in his study. His insight into secular society and his ministry of apologetics were forged between living by faith, growing food for his family, and helping individuals with all sorts of problems who made all sorts of demands upon Schaeffer's home life. Given the circumstances under which he worked and the fact that his insight was perceptive and his ministry effective, Pinnock's comments about Schaeffer's "lack of credible scholarship" and being "beyond his depth" are, sadly, somewhat petty.

CONCLUSION

Even if we accept some error of detail in Schaeffer's writings, his big picture has proven durable. As Michael Hamilton has observed, the "conceptual centerpiece of Schaeffer's historical view is the triumph of relativism in the modern post-Christian world." The advent of "post-modern" thought would not have surprised him, nor "would he have been surprised by the resultant moral vacuum that characterizes much contemporary academic thinking."[142] Indeed it is quite remarkable that in the early 1960s—long before the views of Gadamer were essential reading for every aspiring academic—Schaeffer recognized that all people bring their presuppositions to a text and "read it" from their particular point of view.[143] It was his recognition of the futility of the search by the secular academy for objective truth that marked Schaeffer as a perceptive thinker. Yet unlike the postmodernist slide into cynicism, despair, and nihilism, Schaeffer continued to contend for objective truth and hope—a truth and hope located only in Jesus Christ. Schaeffer was not an academic in the traditional sense, but he was a thinker, and indeed, I would suggest, a thinker with prophetic insight. Hamilton is right to note that Schaeffer "was evangelicalism's most important public intellectual in the 20 years before his death. Ideas were to him literally matters of life and death."[144]

However, of fundamental importance to Schaeffer was the conviction that not only is there a truth that has content and can be verbalized, but this truth has to be lived. He was adamant that in an age that does not believe truth exists, you cannot speak with credibility if you did not practice truth.[145] Indeed, on the basis of John 17:21, he argued that the final apologetic involved relationships between Christians. Schaeffer maintained that you could not expect the world to believe Christianity is true "unless the world sees some reality of the oneness of true Christians."[146] Thus in trying to evaluate the apologetics of Francis Schaeffer, once more we are challenged by the fact that he did not just follow a particular theoretical methodology. Indeed, although his own style of apologetics placed great importance on the role of rational discussion, it was in the practice of truth by Christians that Schaeffer located ultimate importance. Hence in considering Schaeffer's apologetics, any evaluation that attempts to understand him by only examining his books is seriously deficient. Instead of disputing which apologetical school fits Schaeffer, time would be better spent studying the actual manner of *how* he conducted his ministry of apologetics. As stated in previous chapters, for Schaeffer the *manner* of how apologetics is conducted is as important as the *message*. And by manner I mean not only the way Schaeffer conducted the apologetical discussions but the way he lived and related to other Christians.

As Schaeffer himself said in the preface to one of his books, in his apologetics he wanted to deal with the intellectual and cultural questions of the modern person. But he also regarded it as essential that at L'Abri they would "demonstrate that the Personal-Infinite God exists." Both elements had to be kept together in unity, for to separate them "would grieve the Holy Spirit and sever the link with modern man."[147] Visitors to L'Abri talked about "the feeling of well-being which enveloped" them and the reality of prayer as communication with God. As the Schaeffers intended, students visiting often recognized that L'Abri "existed on the basis of prayer, as a demonstration of God's existence."[148] Furthermore, L'Abri sought to model authentic Christian community and to show the reality of relationships among Christians who have experienced substantial healing and a special oneness in Christ. In fact, Schaeffer believed that you could not explain his ministry or the work of L'Abri without reference to the concept of community.[149]

It was this powerful combination of a loving Christian community, rational discussions with individuals, and the reality of God working supernaturally through prayer that made Francis Schaeffer so effective as an apologist. We now live in an age when reason is devalued, and for many people "behind every truth claim is an unacknowledged bid for control and power." In such a situation, the apologetics of Francis Schaeffer with its stress on rationality seems to have little relevance. However, as Burson and Walls argue, sacrificial love, "credibly demonstrated, has as much chance as anything at breaking down the walls of suspicion within which many postmoderns have chosen to shelter themselves."[150] In the concluding chapter we will therefore consider to what extent the apologetics of Francis Schaeffer can still be used as a tool in evangelism.

Conclusion: Love as the Final Apologetic

Is Schaeffer Still Relevant?

After Francis Schaeffer died on May 15, 1984, there was a risk, as James Packer noted, that some of the people at L'Abri would "labor to build the prophet's tomb, embalming into hallowed irrelevance thoughts that were once responses to the desperations of our time."[1] That this did not happen was the result of a deliberate effort by the leadership of the various branches of L'Abri to remain faithful to Schaeffer's original vision. In other words, they sought to welcome visitors who were struggling in one way or another and to come alongside them with the saving love of Jesus Christ. As people came over the succeeding years with new problems, new doubts, and new questions, L'Abri sought to provide new answers rather than merely parroting stock answers to previous questions. By this approach, L'Abri continued to relate to new generations of disillusioned youth struggling with doubts and problems in relation to the Christian faith and Christian life. However, the question now arises, given the fundamental changes in cultural and intellectual attitudes over recent years, as to whether apologetics (with its stress on rationality) has a meaningful part to play in evangelizing people in a postmodern age.

The shift from modernism to postmodernism, which some see as the biggest cultural change since the Enlightenment, has been extremely well (indeed exhaustively) documented and is beyond the scope of this study.[2] Yet, what are relevant to our discussion are the differences in approach and outlook brought about by postmodernism and how these changes impact Christian witness in general and apologetics in particular. Observing the differences that university missions must now face, Don Carson has said that many of "these differences are nothing other than the outworking of one form or another of pluralism, both in the academic world and in the culture at large."[3] However, another evangelical writer, Alister McGrath, finds the problems and difficulties to be with evangelical apologetics itself. He has suggested that evangelicalism has operated within an Enlightenment worldview of universal human rationality. It thus regards evangelism as being about "persuading people of the *truth* of the gospel—with that crucial word 'truth' being understood in a strongly rational manner as propositional correctness."[4] McGrath believes that a strongly rationalist spirit can be discerned within the writings of evangelicals like Carl Henry and Francis Schaeffer in relation to their view of Scripture as well as in their approach to apologetics.

McGrath argues that

> the Enlightenment forced evangelicalism into adopting approaches to spirituality which have resulted in rather cool, detached, and rational approaches to Scripture. The traditional "Quiet Time" has been deeply influenced by this outlook.[5]

McGrath wants to purge evangelicalism of what he sees as its Enlightenment rationalism, and he maintains that the "apologetic and theological adjustment to the decline of modernity" is a priority for evangelicalism.[6] Dave Tomlinson is another critic, but one who would go further than McGrath. He even criticizes Schaeffer for his commitment to biblical inerrancy. Tomlinson, a one-time charismatic evangelical who now describes himself as a post-evangelical, in his book *The Post-Evangelical* said of inerrancy that he simply marveled "that anyone should think it plausible or necessary to believe in such a thing." For him, inerrancy was merely "a rationalist response to a rationalist attack, and it has proved to be one of the most troublesome and divisive pieces of evangelical dogma ever invented."[7] Were we to listen to these critics, we would conclude that not only does Schaeffer's apologetics have no role or future in a postmodern age, but that they do not deserve to have any role in the future. However, the truth is somewhat different.

McGrath himself, in a scathing critique of Tomlinson's book, reveals how ill-informed and inadequately thought through is *The Post-Evangelical*.[8] So we need not rehearse the arguments against Tomlinson or spend time on his theologically naive criticism of Schaeffer. Earlier in this book I dealt with those who regarded Schaeffer's approach as being too rationalist, and elsewhere I deal with McGrath's criticism of the influence of the Enlightenment on evangelicalism in general.[9] Although McGrath is a distinguished scholar who raises serious theological concerns about the Enlightenment, I believe that his understanding of classical evangelicalism is defective. Thus I regard many of the conclusions that he reaches as being inaccurate. Yet, it is quite clear that there has been a genuine and fundamental cultural change. So, do the apologetics of Francis Schaeffer still have relevance? Without hesitation I would argue yes. Indeed, I would suggest that in a postmodern age Schaeffer's approach is even more necessary.

POSTMODERNISM: FRIEND OR FOE?

Postmodernism has, as Stanley Grenz observed, a largely negative orientation in that it "began as a rejection of the modern mind-set launched under the conditions of modernity."[10] Some evangelicals have found the emergence of postmodernism encouraging, and others have even actively welcomed it. Rejecting the idea of any sort of objectivity and rationality, postmodernism argues that all theories, rather than being based on facts, are simply developed to empower those who hold them. Thus for Michael Foucault, a leading postmodernist writer, "truth" is the result of power-relationships that masquerade as neutral means of enforcing order.[11] Yet Grenz finds common ground with postmodernism because of its rejection of Enlightenment epistemology. He feels that "evangelicals have often uncritically accepted the modern view of knowledge despite the fact that at certain points the post-modern critique is more in keeping with Christian theological understandings."[12] However, Grenz is wrong to think that "the enemy of my enemy is my friend." Postmodernism is largely non-theistic and united with modernism in its philosophical naturalism. The leading postmodernist thinkers "deny the objective existence of God and the supernatural, and take the material universe to be all there is."[13]

Furthermore, by arguing not only that all knowing and all speaking is done from a particular perspective, but that each perspective is equally true and valuable, postmodernism promotes not merely an alternative truth but a plurality of truths. And this relativism extends to moral issues. As Douglas Groothuis notes, unlike modernists who "attempted to retain some sense of objective moral values or cross-cultural ethical standards," postmodernists—though they tend to call themselves contextualists—are "moral relativists of one stripe or another."[14] Although some people (including those evangelicals who wish to work with postmodernism) like to view postmodernism as a radical departure from the modernism of the Enlightenment, it is in many ways nothing more than "modernism gone to seed, carried to its logical conclusions and inevitable demise."[15] Long before most evangelicals had ever heard of Foucault, Francis Schaeffer had spotted a 1966 review of his book *Madness and Civilisation* and recognized the significance of what Foucault was saying. For those who suggested that Schaeffer's example of secular thought was unimportant because it was so "totally extreme," Schaeffer, with prophetic insight, argued that Foucault is "not too isolated to be of importance in understanding our era." Indeed, as Schaeffer predicted and as events would confirm, the "logical end of the dichotomy, in which hope is separated from reason, is the giving up of all reason."[16]

As Groothuis has noted, postmodernism "is not only an overreaction to the true but exaggerated elements of modernism; it is also an exaggeration of the false elements in modernism."[17] Thus, far from welcoming postmodernism or even wanting to work with it, evangelical Christians need to confront it. It is no friend of the Christian faith, and it needs to be opposed. I believe that Don Carson is correct in his assessment that "philosophical pluralism is the most dangerous threat to the gospel since the rise of the Gnostic heresy in the second century."[18]

Millard Erickson has criticized writers such as David Wells for condemning trends in secular thought but then failing to provide practical advice on how to reverse such trends.[19] The same cannot be said of Francis Schaeffer. I am convinced that his apologetics provides a model that enables us not only to condemn but to oppose postmodernism. And not only to oppose it for the sake of opposing it, but to minister to individuals influenced by postmodernism (and thus blinded to their true spiritual state) so they will be led to a saving faith in Jesus Christ.

A LOVE FOR THE INDİVİDUAL

Schaeffer had a love for people that underpinned and inspired his apologetics. He had a concern for the individual person and a real burden for those separated from the saving love of Jesus Christ. It was a love that led Schaeffer to inconvenience himself and his family time and time again for the sake of the other person. Writing to a friend in 1953, two years before L'Abri was formally established, Schaeffer stated that "with so many people coming down our little path, it makes a severe problem," but "talking about the things of the Lord always comes first, and when someone comes who wants to know about the Lord, all other things must wait."[20] This concern for individual people continued throughout his ministry, and even in the 1970s when he addressed meetings of four thousand and five thousand people, individuals mattered. Burson and Walls tell how, just after he had spoken to four thousand people, Schaeffer displayed "remarkable patience and compassion" with a man suffering from cerebral palsy who asked long and nearly incoherent questions.[21]

This sort of love and compassion speaks volumes to people. And people are quick to recognize whether it is genuine or merely a mask we wear while on duty doing our professional Christian ministry or engaged in apologetics. Schaeffer loved people, he cared deeply for individuals, and he was passionate about reaching them with the gospel of Jesus Christ. Indeed as he himself said, "If we fight our philosophic battles . . . coolly without emotional involvement, do we really love God?"[22] Schaeffer knew God—His love, His truth, and His holiness. Yet looking at his own country and the Western world, he realized how it now trampled on what God had given and thus was under the judgment of God. For Schaeffer, as with Jeremiah, this was a time for tears. He believed that "we must cry for the poor lost world, for we are all of one kind."[23]

For Schaeffer, having love for the lost also meant confronting them about their sin and the need for repentance. From his experience of dealing with many unchurched and disillusioned young people, he found that if they could "feel real compassion in you," they were willing to listen to what you had to say.[24] Schaeffer was uncompromising about what needed to be said to individuals, but as one former L'Abri student noted:

> [T]he rigor of his convictions was always tempered with love and understanding in person-to-person relationships as well as in public debate. He invariably treated those with whom he deeply disagreed with consideration and love.[25]

Unlike other types of apologetical argument, which are marshaled with polemical venom, Schaeffer demonstrated how "apologetics must be saturated with compassion and pastoral wisdom if the message is to be attractive."[26] For those of us living in the West during the twenty-first century, with all its biblical illiteracy, philosophical pluralism, and moral relativism, having a real love for the individual is an essential prerequisite for effective evangelism.

Yet even during the late 1960s, which was the heyday of intense philosophical discussion at L'Abri, it was Schaeffer's love and compassion that often won over many individuals. Sylvester Jacobs, an African-American who had been treated badly in the United States, even by those professing to be Christian, found that he and Schaeffer could "talk to one another as human beings."[27] Years after his visit to L'Abri (where he met his wife Janet), Jacobs recalls going for a hike in the mountains with Schaeffer. Struggling with difficult issues (for example, does God really care for black people?) and wrestling with painful emotions (including bitterness), Jacobs asked several searching questions that Schaeffer sought to answer. However, what really spoke to Sylvester Jacobs was the realization that this was Schaeffer's day off, and he had invited Jacobs to be with him. Thinking of Edith Schaeffer,

Jacobs remembers her as being like a mother figure: "I think of her as someone who cares, someone who loves me. She was part of my life in a very special way."[28]

LOVE MADE THE DIFFERENCE

This genuine concern for people and the sense of love for the individual that the Schaeffers had, was, as one long-term worker at L'Abri noted, "what made the difference."[29] What has been called their "pastoral touch" was not merely some professional skill they exercised as part of their paid ministry. The love they displayed for individuals sprang from deep within their hearts, and that gave it an authenticity that was compelling. Francis Schaeffer, with all his commitment to rational apologetics, remained convinced that love between Christians was "the final apologetic."[30] Love and truth went together, and truth was never to be an abstract intellectual concept. Indeed Schaeffer argued that Christians must not merely speak about truth—they must practice it. He knew that in a skeptical age influenced by relativism, Christian apologetics with its claim to absolute truth would not be taken seriously if Christians did not live out the truth.[31]

Again, we need to emphasize that the love being displayed by the Schaeffers was not just a tool being used to commend their apologetics. Indeed I would maintain that the apologetics of Francis Schaeffer flowed from his love for people. Furthermore, it is clear that long before he engaged in a ministry of apologetics he (and Edith) had a deep love for individuals. Back in 1941–1943 when he was an associate pastor at a church in Chester, Pennsylvania, a family had a child with Down's syndrome. The parents could not afford to give the boy a special education, and so Schaeffer, in addition to his normal duties, went twice a week with colored blocks in a variety of shapes and patiently taught him.[32] This is true Christian love—a compassion for those considered by society to be unimportant and a compassion that is costly in terms of time, effort, and commitment.

Do we see compassion and love like this today in many churches? Can the outsider visit your church and experience the reality of Christ's love and truth both being taught and lived? And what of our individ-

ual lives—do they reflect the love of Christ, and do we, in an age of
doubt, commend His truth? We each have to start where we are, and
for many that may initially involve asking the Lord to give us a greater
love for other people and a willing spirit to serve and care for others.
As churches, before we can meaningfully reach out with the love of
Christ, we may need to learn how simply to welcome people, to have
a concern for others that enables us to leave our comfort zone and reach
out with a word of welcome to the stranger, to be willing to be incon-
venienced for the sake of others and above all for the sake of the gospel.
It has now been over twenty years since Francis Schaeffer died, but
there is still much we can learn from how he and Edith manifested
Christ's love with a real compassion for individual people. And given
the growing cynical selfishness of secular society, there is an even
greater need for an authentic display of sacrificial love from the followers of Christ.

HONEST ANSWERS TO HONEST QUESTIONS

Schaeffer believed that loving a person involved being willing to give
honest answers to honest questions. Conscious that each generation
had its own particular questions and aware, from his own experience,
that not every intellectual question is a moral dodge to avoid responsibility for sin, Schaeffer argued that there was a real need for somebody
to provide an answer. Schaeffer encouraged those Christians who felt
inadequate to deal with questions to "begin to listen with compassion,
ask what this man's questions really are and try to answer."[33] Having
served as a pastor among ordinary working-class people, Schaeffer
maintained that shipyard workers "have the same questions as the university man. They just do not articulate them in the same way."
Schaeffer did not confuse providing answers with salvation in itself, for
he recognized the necessity of the Holy Spirit's bringing the person to
accept Christ as Savior. Nevertheless, he believed that answering questions helped clear away the obstacles preventing persons from seeing
their need of salvation. Thus Christians had the responsibility to "have
enough compassion to pray and do the hard work which is necessary
to answer the honest questions."[34]

Conclusion: Love as the Final Apologetic

Whatever else the critics may say about Schaeffer, his ministry, or his apologetics, no one can suggest that he lacked compassion or a willingness to do hard work. He made himself available to people, he sought to understand their difficulties (be they intellectual, emotional, or relational), and he attempted to share the truth of Christ in a relevant way. And we should do likewise. In the 1950s when Francis and Edith Schaeffer began the ministry at L'Abri, their approach to individuals was literally revolutionary. It was quite unique to have a place where you could ask any question, where doubt could be handled sensitively, where personal problems could be addressed and the gospel of Jesus Christ applied in a faithful manner. With the radical social upheavals of the 1960s, the rejection of traditional values, the questioning of all authority, and the widespread disillusionment among young people, Schaeffer's approach struck a chord with many. No wonder that from 1968 L'Abri was almost constantly overwhelmed with a throng of young people who despaired of institutional religion but who still sought some meaning to life.[35]

Overwhelmed by large numbers of visitors and distracted in the late 1970s with a focus on other ministries, L'Abri may for a time have lost sight of the importance of providing answers to individuals struggling with Christianity. The introduction of one-to-one instruction in the 1980s at the various branches of L'Abri signaled a renewed importance in its ministry to individuals. Designed to complement group discussion around the meal table, these individual tutorials allowed people the opportunity to ask questions or deal with problems of a more relational nature. Introducing personal instruction has enabled L'Abri to minister effectively to individuals as the type of questions being asked has changed. Applications to visit L'Abri remain high at all its branches, and new branches continue to be established. So clearly the willingness to provide honest answers to honest questions remains attractive.

WILLING TO LISTEN?

For those of us living and witnessing outside the L'Abri community, a willingness to engage with individuals and to seek to deal with their questions, doubts, and problems still has much to commend it. I never cease to be amazed at just how unwilling many Christians are to engage outsiders, refusing to consider their questions or even to attempt to understand why they have problems with trusting in Christ. I recently attended a major Christian conference in my home province of Northern Ireland. About two thousand people were present, and the Bible teaching by the visiting speaker was excellent. On the last day he conducted a seminar where people could ask questions on any subject. Most questions came from Christians and were about living out the faith, but then one non-Christian queried the biblical account of the resurrection of Jesus Christ. The visiting speaker was outstanding in his handling of the question and followed through with an invitation to chat with him afterward on a one-to-one basis. What was so sad was the way many Christians openly disapproved of the question, murmured, "tut-tut," or even said, "shame." It was clear that for them the conference was a nice religious club of like-minded individuals, and they had no time for outsiders' questions. How different from the ministry of Francis Schaeffer, and how different—more importantly—from the ministry of our Lord Jesus Christ!

If we are serious about reaching the lost (and that perhaps is the first question many Christians need to consider), then we must engage with individuals and the particular questions and problems (be they intellectual or emotional) with which they struggle. Even in what was once religious Northern Ireland, the so-called Bible belt of the United Kingdom, large segments of society now have real doubts about the uniqueness of Jesus Christ, questioning the historical reliability of the Bible accounts of His life, death, and resurrection, rejecting the need for absolute truth as revealed in the Bible, and struggling with the exclusive claims of Christianity as being the only way to salvation. To those who say that we now live in a postmodern society where most people don't ask such questions or seek rational explanations, I want to say, get close to individuals and listen carefully. As you come alongside individual people, as they see that you care about them, as they grasp that you are open to free discussion (and will not think any less of them for raising difficult questions), you will discover that the questions will pour out.

Serving as minister of a church near the Queen's University of Belfast, I deal with a variety of unchurched, skeptical people. In addition to providing a weekly Bible preaching ministry, I attempt each week to meet, on a one-to-one basis, in a local café with two or three individuals who have major problems or doubts about organized religion and to work through the particular questions they have. It has been amazing to see how people respond to these conversations and their subsequent willingness to attend a Christianity Explored course and their openness to the claims of the gospel itself. As you make yourself available for ministry like this, you will discover that it is not just university students who have questions to be answered. You will find yourself speaking with ordinary working people and with individuals of all ages.

Perhaps as an individual you don't feel able to conduct one-to-one conversations with non-Christians about their doubts and problems. If so, why not invite them to a church or a special event where they can have the freedom to ask questions. It is very encouraging to see churches in England, where the preaching of the Bible is taken seriously, also run evangelistic events where people sitting around tables hear a Bible address and afterward take part in small discussion groups while written questions can be given to the speaker. Could your church organize an event like this even if you have to bring in an outside speaker? In the United States, Christian groups have organized the Veritas Forum at a number of universities. The ethos of the forum is not to provide a defense of Christianity but to enable any person to ask any question about the possibility of truth in relation to Jesus Christ.[36] Over one hundred thousand students have become involved in the different forums. So yet again we are reminded that there is still a demand for honest answers to honest questions, and the approach of Francis Schaeffer obviously remains relevant today.

NEW TIMES AND NEW QUESTIONS

Nevertheless, one must recognize that there is not the same demand for the type of heated discussion that there was in the late 1960s. Os Guinness, the well-known Christian writer and speaker, was a student and worker at L'Abri in the late sixties and early seventies. Speaking in 2003 about the ministry of L'Abri during the "hippie era," Guinness recalls, "the key thing was that it was a non-stop passionate discussion about the way things were [in society] and the relevance of the Christian faith."[37] Yet the absence of such passionate discussions does not mean an absence of questions needing to be answered. The 1960s was a revolutionary period in every sense of the word, and passionate discussions about everything and anything were part of that milieu. As is normal with all such periods in history, society soon experienced a collective "settling-down," and there was a social reaction against fervor and enthusiasm for change. With such developments went the demand for passionate discussion.

Furthermore, the rise of pluralism and the triumph (at least in the media and the academy) of a radical tolerance has meant less discussion of competing ideas. As Professor Don Carson observes, there is

less discussion because toleration of diverse ideas demands that we avoid criticizing the opinions of others; in addition, there is almost no discussion where the ideas at issue are of the religious sort that claim to be valid for everyone everywhere.[38]

Os Guinness is correct to point out that "philosophically speaking, pluralism is not in itself relativism and need not entail it."[39] However, in practice this has been applied to mean just that, and thus truth is no longer something to be discovered but instead is something manufactured. For those who hold to relativism, "truth isn't fixed by outside reality, but is decided by a group or individual for themselves."[40] Thus the claims of Christianity are not rejected because they lack truth but "*because* they purport to be true."[41] One survey of American university students found that the most common word used by non-Christians to describe Christians was "intolerant."[42]

Yet, in spite of all that I have just said, I believe that Schaeffer's desire to provide honest answers to honest questions still remains a meaningful and relevant ministry. Why? you might ask. Well, quite apart from the fact that a significant number of people are still willing to go where they can ask meaningful questions (as seen by bookings to

L'Abri and attendance at the Veritas Forums), all people are by nature rational creatures. Thus all persons are capable of rational discourse, and as John Stott has pointed out, "one of the noblest features of the divine likeness in man is his capacity to think."[43] However unfashionable it may be to say so, people still have questions about fundamental issues (even if they are not verbalized) because that is how we are made. Confrontational discussions at public venues may not be appropriate today—if indeed they ever were—but engaging individuals on a one-to-one basis is extremely valid. It allows us as Christians to come alongside individuals, to listen to their questions (or even prod them into asking questions), to answer the questions within the framework of their own (defective) worldview, and then to explain a Christian worldview, the need for Christ's saving work, and the reasons why we have accepted the gospel. The questions may be different from those handled by Francis Schaeffer, but the need to provide answers remains every bit as strong. Indeed I would contend that given the current ethos that all truth is relative and all faiths are equal, there is an even greater need for us as Christians to provide honest answers to honest questions.

A TRUTH FOR ALL

The truth choice offered to individuals in contemporary society has effectively reduced truth to one of personal taste. Some writers, such as Stanley Hauerwas, who himself is a Christian, have come to reject, as Curtis Chang points out, "any attempt to ground the church's proclamation in the modernist fiction of a universally acknowledged rationality."[44] He repeatedly emphasizes that it is not the task of the Christian to demonstrate that all other positions are false. Instead, Christians—as the church—must be a "story formed" community. How the church encounters those outside its story is left rather vague, and Hauerwas accepts that his approach leads to a "certain kind of relativism." What makes the claim of the Christian community unique, if anything? And how is the message of the Christian community any more right than, say, the conflicting message of the Mormon community or the Muslim community? And if you try to suggest that an inner spiritual experience has validated the truth of

Christ for you, a Mormon or a Muslim could equally claim authority from a spiritual experience.

For Christians, truth is located in Jesus Christ and in His gospel, and this truth is not just for Christians but for all people everywhere. As Christ Himself said, no one comes to God the Father except through Him (John 14:6). And as John Stott reminds us, "God has revealed himself in *words* to *minds*. His revelation is a rational revelation to rational creatures."[45] Adopting Schaeffer's strategy of providing honest answers to honest questions and doing so on a one-to-one basis in the context of a friendship is an effective way to identify false notions of what is true (and indeed of what is truth) and to clear away obstacles that prevent people from seeing their need for God's saving grace. Working through particular issues, doubts, or problems with individuals allows them to see that coming to a saving faith in Christ is not an irrational experience or a blind leap of faith into the dark. And in an age when people have the choice to take any sort of blind leap in any kind of direction, it becomes even more important (not less) to provide solid rational and coherent reasons as to why Christianity, and it alone, is right and true.

However, it is essential in these one-to-one discussions that we actually listen to the person we are engaged with and endeavor to grasp just what it is that is bothering them or preventing them from being open to the truth-claims of Christianity. If our ministry is to be effective, we need to listen before we speak, so that the answers we offer really do relate to the questions being asked. It might save us a lot of hard work, but serving up pre-prepared answers to questions that the person hasn't actually asked is not going to be productive. Listening to the person, working out an answer that engages him or her, and then seeking to present a Christian worldview will take time and effort. But if we have love for the individual, we will be willing to invest our time and make the effort, both on the intellectual and emotional levels. It is also important that we remember that many intellectual questions actually result from emotional barriers. Thus as Wim Rietkerk, the leader of Dutch L'Abri, has written, "in the process of coming to believe and growing in faith we can flounder when the emotional side of personal being is neglected."[46] Given the greater emphasis today on the emotions and on how we feel, it is all the more necessary that in our apologetics we retain the integration of reason, will, and emotion.

This is not to regard Francis Schaeffer's approach as inadequate or defective, but it does acknowledge the reality that new times bring new emphases as well as new questions. Such an understanding was integral to Schaeffer's own approach. In January 1964 following a visit to the United Kingdom and the United States in December 1963, Schaeffer gave a key lecture in Farel House on the need to be aware of changes in society and to be able to address the changing scene. His visit had caused him great concern that evangelicals were failing to connect with the next generation, and he argued for communication that took account of the new ways of thinking about truth and reality.[47] In this, Schaeffer showed himself able to adapt (and indeed eager to adapt) to a changing situation so that the truth of the gospel of Jesus Christ could be meaningfully shared. Without fossilizing the particular arguments Schaeffer used at a given moment in history, we do well to continue to follow his approach, for then we shall be able to face the new times and new questions that confront the emerging generation.

NEW TIMES AND NO QUESTIONS

Of course some will suggest that the nature and scale of the intellectual and social changes since the 1960s are so radical that the type of apologetics practiced by Schaeffer no longer has any role. Not only have we moved away from the passionate discussion of the 1960s, but most people don't even ask questions or care about the meaning of life. They are simply interested in themselves, in their own lives, and in having a "good time." However, far from being left behind by these new social realities, Francis Schaeffer was tracing them and was adapting his apologetics accordingly. As early as 1973 he observed the emergence of a new bourgeoisie from the student radicals of the 1960s. Yes, their lifestyle was very different from the middle classes of their parents' day. Those in the new middle class took drugs, were promiscuous in sexual matters, and were hedonistic. But they upheld the two cardinal values of personal peace and affluence. Schaeffer noted that they wanted "enough personal peace to practice their new life-style," and they "couldn't care less where the affluence comes from. . . . So long as they can afford . . . to do what pleases them, that's enough."[48]

Over the past twenty-five years this has led to a growth of a culture that worships the individual, is obsessed with self-fulfillment, and seeks to find meaning in the self as a substitute for God. As Professor David Wells has noted, life in society is now "characterized by self-righteousness, self-centeredness, self-satisfaction, self-aggrandizement, and self-promotion."[49] Living and seeking to minister in the first decade of the twenty-first century, hedonism rather than existentialism seems to be the main challenge to the Christian gospel. Certainly, serving as I do near a major university and dealing with students and young professionals, I have to say that not many are knocking on my door to ask about the purpose of their life. Instead I come across many who live without moral restraint or thought for other people or any consideration of the broader picture. They encapsulate the person from Ecclesiastes who declared that he denied himself nothing his eyes desired nor refused his heart any pleasure. To talk of apologetics in this situation seems utterly foolish.

Yet the hedonistic lifestyle did not just happen, and behavior does not just happen in a vacuum. Hedonism in itself is a set of beliefs (however basic and undeveloped) that then affect and govern behavior. Some folk who pursue a hedonistic lifestyle may have come to realize just how empty and ultimately how unfulfilling it is. And like the person in Ecclesiastes, they may have come to hate life because all of it is meaningless, "a chasing after the wind" (Eccl. 1:17, NIV). It is no wonder that social commentators talk about a growing sense of disillusionment and despair among young people, nor sadly surprising that youth suicides have risen alarmingly. Forty years ago, speaking to students and workers at L'Abri, Francis Schaeffer warned that suicide was the logical outcome for those knowingly living without meaning and who had descended into the blackness of irrationality.[50] To those standing on the brink of suicide, Schaeffer argued in this lecture that Christians must reach out and offer the true hope of the gospel. His apologetics seemed an effective means for connecting with such disillusioned people, and they remain so today. Yet for those living a hedonistic lifestyle but who recognize its ultimate emptiness, many more are living in ignorance or denial of this reality. If they are quite happy with their lives and have no profound questions, can the apologetics of Francis Schaeffer play a role?

I believe the answer is yes. For if people are not asking questions, then we must be willing to ask them the questions they need to consider. One of the distinctive features of Schaeffer's approach was his tactic of following the person's values and presuppositions (even when the person has hitherto been unaware of them) to their logical conclusion. Convinced that no one could in reality live out these non-Christian presuppositions, Schaeffer wanted to find a point of tension within each person that forced him or her to question his or her own values. I agree with Schaeffer that many people do not so much reject Christianity as fail to even consider it because of their presuppositions (however hidden they may be), and therefore they need to be challenged. Apart from those who have gained their presuppositions unconsciously from the society around them, Schaeffer also recognized that some individuals try to bury themselves in themselves, for "down inside of himself, man finds it easy to lie to himself."[51]

LIFTING THE ROOF OFF

Schaeffer realized that pushing persons toward the logical conclusion of their presuppositions and finding their point of tension would cause them pain. Nevertheless, he maintained that we must "have the courage to lift the roof off other people's lives and expose them to the collapse of their defences."[52] People can live in denial of reality and build a life full of false psychological props or intellectual props (or these days anti-intellectual props) or sociological props, all of which are designed to give a false sense of meaning or a fleeting feeling of satisfaction. Taking away these props would be utterly cruel but for one reason, and "that is because it is true. There is a hell. There is nobody in all history who has been so cruel as Jesus Christ unless truly men are lost and going to hell."[53] And thinking about the awfulness of hell should likewise inspire within us a new love for the lost and motivate afresh our pre-evangelistic and evangelistic witness. Love for the individual must remain real throughout our discussion. As Schaeffer wisely observed, "As I push the man off his balance, he must be able to feel that I care for him."[54]

It is my experience from ministry that using Schaeffer's approach to generate questions and to unsettle the individual can be a very helpful tool for engaging those who appear to be quite content to live their lives without reference to God. And I agree with Schaeffer that once a person has come to see his or her real situation and his or her need of God's saving grace, there is no need to be complicated. For in sharing the gospel "not only can the same ideas be given, but even the same words can be used to all men."[55] Of course, not every person we expose to his (or her) point of tension will be willing for the true solution. Consequently, we

> may seem to leave him in a worse state than he was in before. But this is the same as the evangelism of the past. Whenever the evangelist preached the reality of Hell, men who did not believe were more miserable after hearing the preaching than if they had never heard him.[56]

No one would willingly want to leave a person like this, and indeed our whole desire is for him or her to receive Christ as Lord and Savior. However, we must be extremely careful not to forget that only God through His Holy Spirit can regenerate people. Our task is just to present His gospel in such a way that it is properly understood.

HONESTY OR CYNICISM?

Pushing people to their particular point of tension relies upon being able to challenge them about their individual lack of intellectual consistency. I suspect that some readers will remain unconvinced about the effectiveness of such an apologetics weapon in an age that devalues reason. And to an extent that is true (if one may even talk of the truth with such confidence in an era of personal relativism!). However, Dick Keyes, who for many years has led L'Abri Fellowship in Massachusetts, has replaced the term *consistency* with *honesty*. Thus, while continuing to use Schaeffer's style of apologetics, he has, as Burson and Walls observe, "accurately identified the popular sympathies of our postmodern age, and we applaud his attempt to adopt this method accordingly."[57] Keyes has much more extensive experience of ministry among students than I have, and I have no doubt that he has dealt with student bodies in Harvard who are much more radicalized in their postmodernism than are those in Belfast. The fact that he has been able to successfully engage these students (and other cynical and selfish young adults) and find a real opening for the truth-claims of Christianity is a great encouragement. It has given us the confidence to use Schaeffer's approach in this day and age, and I too can confirm that we have found it still to be an effective tool for apologetics.

The switch from stressing *consistency* to *honesty* may not seem like much, but I believe it enables us to penetrate the mind-set of the contemporary selfish, hedonistic, and relativist individual. When you point out to such a person that he is not logical in his views nor, in his lifestyle, consistent in his own values, he may just shrug his shoulders (as indeed some have done with me) and say, "So what?" However, when you challenge a person about failing to be honest and not being true to himself and continue to unpack this in terms of his not therefore being authentic as a person, you do tend to get under his skin. Again, as Francis Schaeffer warned, we must be careful not to cause unnecessary pain or to be offensive; yet in wanting to lift the roof off, our aim is to disturb the complacent and spiritually indifferent person. The widespread relativism and apathy that prevail may be dressed up in postmodern clothes, but people have attempted to divert themselves from the big questions of life in various ways since the Fall. Francis Schaeffer recognized that "most people in our society simply have been carried along by the cultural consensus." He wanted to show them— and so must we—that "there is too much at stake in life to buy into any worldview, including Christianity, without adequate reflection."[58]

CONTENDING FOR TRUE TRUTH

Lifting the roof off an individual's life and challenging his or her lack of personal truth or authenticity is, as I have already mentioned, an effective means of connecting with those who were previously spiritually indifferent or complacent. Yet, to fail to move from the question of personal truth to objective truth and not to present the reality of the Christian worldview would only trap us in a relativist cul-de-sac. Certainly there is nothing wrong with understanding and engaging a culture on its own terms and modifying our apologetics accordingly. However, while it is true that "objective truth may not be the most fruitful point of entry in contemporary apologetics, it cannot be ignored or soft-pedalled in the long run without disastrous consequences."[59] Speaking in January 1964, Schaeffer perceived that the central battle for the new generation would revolve around the fact "that we are dealing with content and truth and we are not dealing merely with existential experience."[60]

Prophetic though Schaeffer's interpretation of cultural trends was, I doubt if he realized at that point just how much evangelicalism (or a substantial segment of it) would be influenced by the new intellectual climate. Many evangelical writers—seeing postmodernism as the vanquisher of modernity and its Enlightenment values—have rushed to embrace postmodernism. Thus Stanley Grenz says that he is in "fundamental agreement with the post-modern rejection of the modern mind" with its assumption that "knowledge is certain, objective and good."[61] For Grenz, truth is social—i.e., the product of the community of which the knower is a part. Not only are the specific truths we accept conditioned by the group or community we belong to, but so too is the very conception of truth. Hence, as Millard Erickson points out, for postmodernists "truth is relative to that community."[62]

Grenz also laments that evangelical presentations of the gospel have been "accompanied by a rational apologetic that appeals to proofs for the existence of God, the trustworthiness of the Bible, and the historicity of Jesus' resurrection."[63] While noting that evangelical systematic theologies have generally focused on the propositional content of the faith, Grenz argues that we must "rethink the function of assertions of truth or propositions." He believes that the evangelical understanding of the Christian faith "must not remain fixated on the propositionalist approach."[64] Clark Pinnock is also very critical of the previous emphasis on propositional theology and wishes to develop a narrative theology. In his approach, the task of theology is to help tell the Christian story, and he suggests that "doctrines that help us understand the story better are good and true; doctrines that ruin and distort the story are false and harmful."[65] Within his new theological approach, Pinnock believes there should be room for liberal "Christians to relate contemporary stories," while conservative Christians can "rehearse the mighty deeds of God."

The fact that what he calls "liberal Christians" are actually anti-evangelical and have a conflicting story to that which the evangelicals want to proclaim is not properly addressed. But then the fact that I am raising the whole issue of objective truth would, sadly, probably lead people like Grenz and Pinnock to label me as nothing more than a prisoner of Enlightenment epistemology. To be fair to Grenz, he does recognize and oppose the postmodern rejection of the correspondence theory of truth (the belief that truth consists of the correspondence of propositions with the world "out there"). He acknowledges that this "not only leads to a skepticism that undercuts the concept of objective truth in general; it also undermines Christian claims that our doctrinal formulations state objective truth."[66]

Yet other writers from the new-style post-conservative evangelical stable, such as Philip Kenneson, appear to have no difficulty giving up on objective truth or the correspondence theory of truth. Since Kenneson does not believe that human beings can take a "view from nowhere," truth cannot be "out there" since it cannot exist independently of the human mind. He views truth-claims as being "inseparably bound up with human language and are, therefore, inextricably linked to matters of discernment and judgment, which means they are irreducibly social or communal affairs."[67] But how do we share "our truth" with those outside "our community"? And why should anyone want to choose our truth-claim (other than personal taste) if there is no basis upon which it can be evaluated against all the other (and competing) truth-claims? Indeed, as James Sire has asked, why should anyone believe anything at all?

THE IMPORTANCE OF RATIONALITY

Of course in reality everyone believes in something, and everyone, at some point or other, uses their human rationality (no matter how rudimentary) to evaluate their belief when challenged. Whether it is our choice of football team, political party, or religion, there are reasons that guide our choice and a rational reflection (albeit in varying degrees) with an evaluation of reality that informs our decision. Universal human rationality is not an Enlightenment assumption; it is part of being human. Likewise, the correspondence theory of truth is not an invention of the Enlightenment. It may have been formalized as a philosophical theory during the Enlightenment, but it simply expresses how people live, consider reality, and deal with the world as it is. Even the skeptical philosophers who disputed the reliability of the senses tended to duck down when walking through a low doorway! They could not live out in the reality of life what they claimed to believe. By contrast, the correspondence theory of truth allows us to match the truth of belief with the truth of reality. And as we deal with individuals today, living in this so-called postmodern age, we discover afresh that in practice they believe in objective truth and the correspondence theory of truth, even if they have never heard of them.

Schaeffer was quite clear that truth must be non-contradictory and must give an answer to the phenomenon in question. Furthermore, one should be able to live consistently with one's truth-claim. In the case of Christianity, one can ask, does it "conform to and explain what we observe concerning man as he is (including any knowledge of myself as a man)?"[68] Schaeffer made much use in his apologetical discussions of the claim that the truth of Christianity is true to what is there in life. Christianity, he argued, is "not only true to what God has said in the Bible, but it is also true to what is there."[69] He maintained that the claims of Christianity were "exactly in line with the experience of every man" and that God acts in the world in a way that "confirms both my observations of the world, and also the way God says it is in the didactic portions of the Bible."[70] I believe that we would do well to continue to follow Schaeffer's approach rather than be swept along by those wanting to embrace postmodernism. I fear that too many of the "open evangelicals" or "post-conservative evangelicals" or those in the "emerging church movement" approach postmodernism on the basis that it is an ally in the fight against modernity. However, like Schaeffer, I tend to view what has now become known as postmodernism as merely a development of modernity, and I believe that its fundamental assumptions are wrong because it continues to ignore the supernatural and merely replaces scientific determinism with cultural determinism.

We should continue to talk about objective truth (that is, truth that is true whether one believes it or not), and we should be unashamedly willing to promote Christianity as *the* truth that all people need to hear and respond to. We need to regain our confidence in the gospel as "true truth," and we need to regain our courage and so be willing to share this gospel with all people. No doubt we shall be accused by society at large and the chattering classes in particular of bigotry and intolerance, but as we work with individual people on a one-to-one basis, we must combine love and truth. In his apologetical discussions, as already mentioned, Schaeffer displayed remarkable patience and compassion, not merely as a tactic but from a genuine concern for the individual. Yet he was adamant that you must emphasize with tremendous force the negative (what you don't mean) before you present the positive message (what you do mean). His reason for urging this approach was to distinguish between the objective truth of content and the subjective truth of existential experience. For Schaeffer, the Bible was "the communication of communicable truth, a communication of rational truth, a truth which can be communicated in words which are understood to be meaningful."[71] It was a content that dealt with real events in history and as such, unlike the experience of existentialism, was open to verification. If we are to confront moral and spiritual relativism, we too must be willing to be negative and criticize that which is wrong and false so as to distinguish and commend the positive message of what is right and true. In Athens Paul did not offer the members of the Areopagus another god but the true "God who made the world and everything in it" (Acts 17:24). So must we.

Each Person Is Unique

Yet in contending for what Schaeffer called "true truth," we must not enjoy it like a game or a kind of intellectual exercise. That would be cruel, and as Schaeffer warned, we could "expect no real spiritual results."[72] There must be a real empathy with the person and a proper relational and emotional dimension to the discussion. Some contemporary apologists want to give such an emphasis to the relational side that they talk about a "person-centered approach" and accept that they can "remain open to the instruction of my dialogue partner."[73] Schaeffer's approach was very person-sensitive, but it was not person-centered, and neither should we become person-centered. We should always aim to win the person for Christ. We want to share the truth with sensitivity and love and in the context of a meaningful relationship, but with the fundamental purpose of leading someone into a relationship with Jesus Christ. It is good to see that the new generation of L'Abri leaders continues to combine Schaeffer's commitment to love and truth.

Jerram Barrs, who is the Resident Scholar of the Francis Schaeffer Institute at Covenant Seminary in St. Louis, has written a major book on evangelism (*The Heart of Evangelism*). While encouraging Christians to reach out to the lost with the gospel, he urges us to treat each person as a unique individual and to be mindful that "every individual we meet is at a different stage in his or her spiritual journey."[74] In his book *If Only I Could Believe!* Wim Rietkerk, who led Dutch L'Abri, and in his book *Beyond Identity* Dick Keyes, who leads the L'Abri community in Southborough, Massachusetts, both give full recognition to the importance of relationships and addressing the emotions.[75] Both remain committed to the concept of objective truth and to contending for the truth of Christ's gospel, but both display a sympathy for the brokenness of individuals and an awareness of barriers that can hold people back.

We need to recognize, as we contend for the truth of Christ's gospel and try to persuade individuals of the importance of accepting its truth-claims, that people are not logical machines or mini Mr. Spocks, devoid of emotions. Thus we may "win" the argument with someone about the truthfulness of Christianity, but they may hold back for a variety of reasons, one of which may be emotional ties to non-Christian family or friends. I have seen this happen when we have tried to reach international students in our city. Some will come, after a few sessions of apologetics or Bible studies, to recognize Jesus Christ as the Son of God and as the only way to know God the Father but draw back from receiving Him as Lord and Savior. The more we get to know the individuals, the more we discover that it is because of emotional and relational factors that they are holding back. Once again, I think we can learn from Francis Schaeffer in this regard.

In 1962 when leading a Bible study in Milan, Schaeffer spoke to a student from a devout Roman Catholic family who had become an evangelical Christian and told her, "If one day you have to leave home, you know that you can have a family with us." When she later had to leave her family, Maria found a second home at L'Abri, where the Lord used the Schaeffers "to bring stability and love back" into her life. Even years later she could "remember vividly the feelings of well-being" that enveloped her at L'Abri.[76] Not many of us may be able literally to take people into our family home, but can we, along with other members of our church, treat outsiders and new members like part of the church family? To the person wanting to leave another faith or to the person struggling to break free from a homosexual lifestyle, can we offer hospitality, can we show friendship, can we give time simply to be with them, and can we treat the other person as a whole person with whom we share love as well as truth? In other words, are we willing to practice what we preach? In reality, to display such loving friendship, given the limits of our time, may mean we need to cut out some activities so we have time to become good friends with a few people.

A COMMUNITY OF BELIEVERS

It is quite fashionable today to want to describe the local church as a sacred community and to portray it as a place where the seeker can experience the divine transcendence.[77] And a number of evangelical churches have responded to renewed interest in spirituality by wanting to make the point of entry as broad and as easy as possible by enabling a person to enjoy a spiritual experience without having to subscribe to any particular set of doctrinal truths. Thus Bible teaching and rational instruction in the truth of the Christian faith have been replaced to a large extent by efforts to create the "right environment" with subdued lighting, the use of candles or icons, and relaxing (and repetitive) worship and by providing personal space to the individual. Recognizing that there is an unparalleled interest in spirituality but a marked distrust of exclusive truth-claims, some writers suggest that the church has to accept "that post-modern people are more likely to come to faith in Christ through spiritual experience which leads to understanding of doctrine than through prior intellectual assent."[78]

John Drane would contend that a Christianity that "has no place for the mystical and the numinous will not be a relevant gospel for the people of today and tomorrow."[79] And while Stuart Murray acknowledges that doctrinal formulations are "crucial," he believes that the experiential side of Christianity and not doctrine should be the priority. He suggests that "spirituality may be the bridge over which doctrinal truth can be carried."[80] The whole approach being advocated seems to be for churches to become open and welcoming communities where people can experience spirituality, come to have a sense of belonging, and then later develop some understanding of the beliefs involved in the gospel.

I do believe that such an approach would indeed make it easier to draw people into your church, though I have serious doubts about the long-term retention rate. However, on a more fundamental level, is such an approach consistent with biblical Christianity? I think not; nor do I think, given the depth of our sinfulness, that a person can be genuinely converted to Christ through such a superficial approach. As Schaeffer has said, you "cannot have a personal relationship with something unknown," and before a person is ready to become a Christian, he or she must have a proper understanding of the truth.[81] Schaeffer was very comfortable with the experiential side of Christianity, but he was always keen to point out that "the Biblically-based experience rests firmly on truth. It is not only an emotional experience, nor is it contentless."[82] I believe that a religious or spiritual experience that is not grounded in biblical truth owes more to Hinduism or Buddhism than to biblical Christianity. It is no coincidence that since Eastern mysticism has become popular in the West, people have been more ready to accept the anti-rational ethos of postmodernism. Indeed, as Professor Don Carson

has said, the new emphasis of the emerging church movement appears
to constitute "a drift toward abandoning the gospel itself."[83]

CONFRONTING IRRATIONAL SPIRITUALITY

In his day Francis Schaeffer recognized the irrationality of existential
experience as a fundamental threat to biblical Christianity, which was
a truth with content. He believed that we could not ignore existentialism but needed to understand the battle so Christians could speak into
it. And even if the Christian message was "an antithesis contrary to the
whole flow of twentieth century thought," it was an antithesis that was
valid.[84] In our day we too must recognize the fundamental threat of an
irrational postmodern spirituality and confront it rather than seeking
to accommodate it within the evangelical church. The apostle Paul
lived and served Christ in an age when people had every sort of spiritual experience to choose from. Yet in the Book of Acts we see that his
approach to evangelism, while culturally sensitive, was always to share
the truth of the gospel. As he preached, he "reasoned" and "explained"
with the aim of "trying to persuade" them to believe the truth.[85]

As John Stott has said, the

> New Testament shows preaching and teaching as working towards a
> decision and it isn't just a case of conversion. They want people to
> trust Christ as He is trustworthy. They argue that He is unique and
> competent to save. They outline what makes Him competent: the
> incarnation, crucifixion and the resurrection.[86]

To have a Christian spiritual experience must involve the Holy
Spirit, and so the person must be familiar with the truth of the gospel,
for the Holy Spirit is the Spirit of truth (John 14:15-27). As Stott
observes, you "cannot exercise faith if you don't exercise your mind.
For faith to be involved, the mind must understand what it believes."[87]
Schaeffer was concerned that the evangelical church was being influenced by the spirit of the age and "failing to recognize that an antithesis exists." He believed that the central antithesis of the Christian faith
was "the antithesis between being justified and not justified."[88]

He contended for the need to stress thesis against antithesis—to point out truth against what was false so that the person could realize the real difference between salvation and being lost. Schaeffer was often criticized for not just preaching the "simple gospel," but as he frequently pointed out, if someone knocks on your door and asks you, "How can I be saved?" in that case you don't discuss presuppositions, you "tell him the gospel. Tell him how Jesus died for him."[89] For Schaeffer, the problem was not the gospel but "how to communicate the gospel so that it is understood."[90] Visiting the English branch of L'Abri at several points during the 1990s, it was encouraging to see a ministry continue and develop Schaeffer's vision. A real effort had been made by Ranald Macaulay, Jock McGregor (now at the Rochester L'Abri), and Andrew Fellows to understand postmodernism, to be able to come alongside individuals influenced or confused by it, while still retaining a total commitment to the importance of sharing doctrinal truths such as biblical inerrancy and substitutionary atonement. This is a refreshing contrast with those in the "emerging church movement" who are willing to tone down the traditional doctrinal understanding so as to make Christianity more attractive to the postmodernist.[91]

THE IMPORTANCE OF COMMUNITY

Having stressed how utterly essential it is that we share unashamedly the truth of the gospel with individuals and confront irrational spirituality, I also want to emphasize the importance of the local church as a community. I do agree with Drane on this point: "in a world of dysfunctional relationships in which people are hurting and constantly being put down . . . many are desperately searching for a place where they can belong and be valued."[92] It is a sad reflection upon a society obsessed with sex that people are now desperate for intimacy and love. But then as John Stott has said, the capacity for relationships is part of the divine likeness in man, whereby we are "made to love. To love other people, and above all, to love God."[93] And the local church as a community of believers should afford us the opportunity to love and be loved, in relation both to God and to other people.

Long before it became so fashionable to talk of the church as a community or the importance of Christian community in itself, Schaeffer gave a strong emphasis to the concept of community. As Burson and Walls note, some of his "most passionate writing revolved around this topic," and even one of Schaeffer's strongest critics, Jack Rogers, found the "description of life at L'Abri exhilarating."[94] For Schaeffer the local church should have "two orthodoxies: first, an orthodoxy of doctrine and second, an orthodoxy of community."[95] Indeed he regarded the sense of a real community as one of the true marks of the early church, and in his study of the Bible, the church at Antioch was his favorite. As Schaeffer noted, it "was a place where something new happened," and "on the basis of the blood of Christ and the truth of the Word of God" believers from different racial, ethnic, and social backgrounds were united as one.[96] Schaeffer believed that Christ's command for Christians to love our neighbors meant "treating every man we meet well, every man whether he speaks our language or not, every man whether he has the colour of our skin or not." Thus there was to be a beauty in human relationships, and much more so in "the relationships between true Bible-believing Christians, something so beautiful that the world would be brought up short."[97] Furthermore, Schaeffer observed that John 17:21 was a sobering thought in that "Jesus gives the world the right to judge whether the Father has sent the Son on the basis of whether the world sees observable love among all true Christians."[98]

DEVELOPING A TRUE COMMUNITY

Yet as Schaeffer looked at the various evangelical churches, he had to conclude that many were little more than "preaching points and activity generators." And if a person really has desperate needs, does "he naturally expect to find a supporting community in our evangelical churches? We must say with tears, many times no!"[99] While recognizing that there cannot be perfection this side of eternity, Schaeffer nevertheless maintained that under the shed blood of Christ there is to be "a substantial healing of everything that the Fall brought forth." One of those things is the division between people, and so the church, by God's grace, was to show that "in a substantial way these can be healed."[100] But Schaeffer was honest enough to admit that all "too often young people have not been wrong in saying the church is ugly."[101] He believed that unless the church practiced the truth as well as talking about it, secular society—which was so skeptical about the concept of truth—would not take Christians seriously. There needed to be beauty and observable love in the relationships between Christians, and that needed to be expressed in the local church as a community.[102]

Through L'Abri, Schaeffer attempted to model what a Christian community should be like. In the 1950s when he and Edith opened their home and simultaneously sought to offer truth and love in a relational context, it was literally a revolutionary approach for someone from an evangelical background to do so. Fifty years later the L'Abri community remains a very powerful witness to both the skeptical unbeliever and the troubled believer. And yet it is a costly business to have a sense of community, and the Schaeffer family paid a heavy price, not only in terms of lack of privacy or normal family life but also in the destruction of their property. For example, in about the first three years of L'Abri, all their wedding presents were wiped out.[103] Perhaps it is the realization to visitors of this very high cost, in every sense, that helps give Christianity at L'Abri the sense of reality.

Speaking of Christian young people from very comfortable families who lacked a sense of spiritual reality, Schaeffer said that if they "saw their parents opening . . . their homes at expense to their furniture and rugs, if they were told to pray not merely for the lost out there somewhere, but for specific people whom they knew sitting at the table in their own home, the unreality could be gone."[104] Schaeffer was always quick to acknowledge the imperfections and weaknesses of L'Abri, but he felt that if it, and the church, was a "little bit of what it should be, young people will come."[105] Individuals, no matter how unusual or "far-out," have always been made welcome at L'Abri and accepted for who they are. Alongside the sense of community involving the L'Abri workers and their families, and the display of concern for the visiting students, there is the presentation of biblical truth through one-to-one instruction, table discussion, lectures, and preaching at Sunday services. Truth has not been abandoned or diminished for the sake of relationships or experience.

THE CHALLENGE TO US

Schaeffer wrote *The Church at the End of the Twentieth Century* and *The Church Before the Watching World* in 1970 and 1971. Some thirty-five years later, we need to ask in humility whether the evangelical church reflects any more faithfully the biblical picture of the church as a community. If we were to score each evangelical church on a scale of 1 to 10 for how good relationships are and how meaningful the sense of community is, I suspect that most would only merit a 2 or 3. Far from providing beauty in relationships, some will be riddled by division and jealousy; far from providing acceptance to the outsider, many will not even give a word of welcome to the visitor; and far from being places of transforming love, many will only reflect the shallow, superficial, and selfish relations of secular society. I said we need to ask in humility about the condition of the church, for given that we are a part of the church, we share a responsibility and bear some of the blame for its shortcomings.

The challenge for us is to be willing to structure our own church as a place for community and, while staying within the limits of the New Testament, to "have the courage to change all kinds of things in our service."[106] Are we even willing to open our own homes as places of community? Most of us probably cannot have people stay, but are we willing to have the person for a meal? A little hospitality and a sharing of our family time can mean so much to a person who lives alone or who is a visitor to our city or a new member of our church. Is your home a fortress or a place for ministry? And if for genuine reasons we can't have people in our homes, are we willing to greet a stranger at church, to help integrate a new member by showing real friendship, or to support an existing member who is struggling with illness or an emotional problem? Surely none of us are incapable of giving a friendly word or delivering a meal to someone in need. If we are to make a difference and if we are to practice community, then as we said before, we will need to review our existing time commitments. We must be willing to cut out meaningless church activities imposed on us by tradition or social expectation, and we must individually be willing to sacrifice some of the leisure time presently reserved and restricted to ourselves.

Many people in our society are suffering, and many Christians feel unsupported and unable to seek help in their local church. I have come across Christians from conservative evangelical churches with excellent expository preaching *and* those from charismatic churches that have brilliantly arranged worship services but who have not experienced love, acceptance, or even real interest in them as individuals. Something is wrong, and—as we have already mentioned—if love is the final apologetic as Schaeffer claimed on the basis of John 17:21, then the evidence of its absence from most evangelical churches is unlikely to attract many people. Perhaps in repentance we need to turn to God and cry out to Him to send His Holy Spirit to stir up in us a new love for Him and for His people.

THE SPIRITUALITY OF SCHAEFFER

For a man so identified with rational apologetics, it is worth recalling that Schaeffer regarded his spiritual crisis of 1951 and the subsequent lectures he prepared on true spirituality as the essential foundation for the work of L'Abri. As he himself said in the Preface to *True Spirituality*, it was "out of these struggles that the reality came, without which an incisive work like L'Abri would not have been possible." He came to see the need for reality as a Christian in the present life on the basis of the finished work of Christ. Lamenting the previous lack of reality in his own life and in the lives of many other Christians, he asked Edith

> what would happen to most churches and Christian work if we awakened tomorrow, and everything concerning the reality and work of the Holy Spirit, and everything concerning prayer, were removed from the Bible. . . . We concluded that it would not make much difference in many board meetings, decisions and activities.[107]

Schaeffer wanted to live and serve in the reality of the supernatural universe, and he argued that this made sense of the biblical image of Christians as "the bride, linking themselves to Christ, the bridegroom, so that He, the crucified, risen, and glorified Christ, may bring forth fruit through them."[108] In practice this meant that "in our thoughts and lives now we are to live as though we had already died, been to heaven, and come back again as risen." Schaeffer felt that if we viewed reality like this, nothing in the world would ever look the same, and the constant pressure to conform would be removed. And we would thus be strengthened in our calling to live in Christ moment by moment and be dead to all things so that "we might be alive to God at this moment."[109] Although Schaeffer held that doctrinal truth was essential, he knew that "it is not an end in itself. There is to be an experiential reality moment by moment."[110] But unlike an existential experience or an experience of the Eastern religions, Schaeffer maintained that the Christian experiential reality was to be enjoyed "with all the intellectual doors and windows open."

Schaeffer recognized that it was a practical problem for individuals to find the point at which they can begin to live moment by moment in this spiritual reality. For him, his own "personal point of beginning was the reality of bringing specific sin under the blood of Christ moment by moment, and knowing the reality of forgiveness and a restored relationship."[111] Whatever the point of beginning for each individual, the aim remained the same: a "moment-by-moment increasing, experiential relationship to Christ and to the whole Trinity."[112] Underpinning all of Schaeffer's rational apologetics was the conviction that the "central doctrine of the Christian faith is not salvation, it is the existence of a personal God who truly is personal in the high order of the Trinity" (i.e., with all the love and communication between the members of the Trinity). Since humankind was made in the image of God, people were made for relationships and, above all, for a spiritual relationship with God.

Substitutionary Atonement

Burson and Walls, while mainly complimentary about Schaeffer's apologetics, are critical of his emphasis on substitutionary atonement as "the only path to divine satisfaction, forgiveness and, consequently, salvation."[113] Although they recognized that there was a relational side in Schaeffer's teaching on salvation, they held that he viewed atonement primarily in legal terms. They also were concerned that if the notion of holiness is "interpreted through a fundamentally forensic grid, this doctrine will naturally appear to be heavily lacquered with a thick tar of legalism. Holiness cannot be reduced to a set of rigid rules without slipping into a tedious and repellent moralism."[114] I agree with Burson and Walls that legalism and moralism are both tedious and repellent. However, at the very heart of Schaeffer's spirituality is the desire that the Christian life not be reduced to "merely a negative not-doing of any small list of things."[115] The spiritual crisis of 1951, described by Edith as a "central event" in his life,[116] forced Francis Schaeffer to confront his legalism and bitterness of spirit. Yet as God worked through it, it also allowed Schaeffer to change and mature, and he never had any desire to return to a legalistic outlook.

Of course, there was an emphasis on substitutionary atonement in Schaeffer's thinking about justification—and there needs to be if one is to be faithful to the teaching of the Bible. But it is wrong to suggest that he viewed salvation mainly in a legal or forensic sense. Schaeffer understood justification to be "absolutely irrevocable" because Christ on the cross took upon Himself the "punishment of all our sin." But the whole purpose of this was to enable the individual to enter a real and meaningful relationship with God when he accepted Jesus Christ as his Lord and Savior. For Schaeffer, salvation was wider than justification, and there was and is a past, a future, and, just as real, a present. He frequently taught that "salvation is not just justification and then a blank until death; God never meant it to be so. Salvation is a unity, a flowing stream, from justification through sanctification to glorification."[117] The reality of salvation at every stage was to be in a loving relationship with God: the freedom to know the Father not just as our Judge but as our loving heavenly Father; to know Christ not just as our Savior but as our bridegroom and brother; and to know the Holy Spirit not just vaguely but as our Comforter who indwells and sustains us.[118]

THE INDWELLING OF THE HOLY SPIRIT

Listening to tapes of his lectures at L'Abri and reading through his letters, one is struck by the constant references to the Holy Spirit and the need for His indwelling power. Long before the charismatic movement burst upon the scene in the 1960s and 1970s, Schaeffer was giving an emphasis (but not an undue emphasis) to the importance of the third member of the Trinity in a manner that was rare within evangelical Christianity. Writing in 1954 to a church leader, Schaeffer said Christians are called "to live in the power of the Holy Spirit in the small as well as large things; to practice doing what the world would consider stupid, in faith that it will please the Lord because it is right."[119] In contrast to the confidence and strength of the secular scientific world, Schaeffer offered a spirituality that emphasized the weakness and the dependence of the individual and his or her utter need of the Holy Spirit. Yet for many people, the authenticity of Schaeffer's spirituality struck a chord and was deeply attractive. For folk visiting L'Abri, the lack of organizational planning to develop the work, the absence of an endowment or financial reserve to fund activities, and the unwillingness to engage in a publicity drive to promote the ministry was a living demonstration of Schaeffer's spiritual reality. The Schaeffers' constant looking to God in prayer to meet the needs of L'Abri, to sustain them in their ministry, and to lead individuals to a saving faith in Christ made a lasting impression on many persons.

I believe that Schaeffer's spirituality is not only biblical but also very wise and indeed relevant. In today's intellectual climate with its suspicion of power, technology, and easy answers, Schaeffer's emphasis on the need of the Holy Spirit should have an even greater appeal among those influenced by postmodernism. Furthermore, given his insistence that true spirituality is not to concentrate on the negative but is finally positive, Schaeffer's spirituality can enhance evangelical Christianity and strengthen its appeal to our contemporary secular society. Schaeffer acknowledged the need for a proper negative aspect to spirituality (i.e., being able to criticize that which is wrong without descending into destructive polemics) but maintained that true spirituality "sweeps over into a positive, and to stop at the negative is to miss the whole point."[120]

Thus Schaeffer's final emphasis on the positive (loving God and loving our neighbor) allows Christians to define themselves by what they are rather than by stressing what they are not. Sadly, too many conservative evangelicals seem to define their self-identity not in terms of the reality of their relationship to the Lord but by what and who they oppose and reject. This can lead to an identity that often is cold, unappealing, and lacking in the fruit of the Spirit. Not only is this spiritually damaging to Christians, but it also undermines the power of their witness. We—and here I include myself—need to be careful lest, in working hard and standing firm against wickedness, we (like the church in Ephesus) forsake our first love and fall from a great height.[121] While many charismatic Christians talk freely of their ongoing relationship with the Lord and appear to have a strong spiritual reality, one sometimes has to question just how biblical their relationship really is. All too often as you take time to listen carefully to how some charismatics describe God, you realize that their understanding draws heavily on their own emotional experience, and their picture of Christ owes more to their own psychological projection than to the biblical revelation. By contrast, Schaeffer's approach to spirituality is based upon the truth of rational understanding of biblical revelation that is then lived out in a moment-by-moment experiential reality.

SPIRITUAL REALITY

Schaeffer's spirituality also affects how we live in relation to other people. Unlike mysticism, which would have us withdraw from everyday life and from contact with people so we can experience "holiness," Schaeffer's approach was geared to help us live out the faith in everyday lives. In *True Spirituality* he gave considerable space to how living in the spiritual reality of our Christian faith should bring "substantial healing" not only to our personal psychological problems, but also in our relationships with other people. Jim Ingram, who was Director of Swiss L'Abri until 2004, used Schaeffer's *True Spirituality* to develop a very effective ministry to individuals struggling with deep emotional problems. By working on a one-to-one basis, he was able to lead confused and hurting believers into a more real and meaningful relationship with the Lord and then deal with issues such as low self-esteem and fractured relations with their family or church. Schaeffer also believed that true spirituality should have a major sociological impact, and when applied to society at large, it should provide the motivation to combat materialistic greed and racist prejudice. He maintained that you "cannot just trample human relationships and expect our relationship to God to be lovely, beautiful and open."[122] Schaeffer held that our spirituality should be real in every aspect of our life, and that should enable us to be involved in every area of society. For him, with his interest in art and music, holiness of life was about being world-redeeming rather than world-denying. It was positive, not negative.

Yet for many of the evangelicals who have come after him with proposals for involvement in politics and social concern, including some who have even claimed an inspiration from Schaeffer himself, there has been a lack of emphasis on true spirituality. Without this emphasis, and also the constant acknowledgment of mankind's depravity, there is a real danger of Christian involvement in these areas being no different from that of other secular special interest groups. Schaeffer realized that with all the different concentric circles you could have for Christian activity and for the faith itself, the innermost circle must always be the spiritual—that is, the "personal relationship of the individual soul with a personal God." Without this, it is not really Bible-believing Christianity.[123] To preserve this innermost circle, Schaeffer regarded prayer as utterly essential. Since the time they became Christians, prayer had always been important to Francis and Edith Schaeffer.

THE PLACE OF PRAYER

Back in the late 1930s, serving in his first church, Schaeffer relied heavily on prayer and in particular on the prayer ministry of a housebound member. He "really felt that her prayers made a tremendous difference in very real situations and had a very real part in our ministry's success."[124] Edith, with her family background in the more pietistic China Inland Mission, had always believed strongly in praying for the provision of particular things or the resolution of particular problems.[125] Following his spiritual crisis in 1951, Francis Schaeffer now also gave a high priority to relying on the Lord through prayer to meet particular material needs. This underpinned L'Abri, and as Schaeffer said in 1964, the life and work of the community was "built upon the concept of prayer."[126] Yet for Schaeffer, the praying for particular needs was only an outworking of the trust there should be in the Lord by His children and only a reflection of the reality of their relationship with the Lord. Coming to God in prayer deepens and strengthens a believer's relationship with God, and Schaeffer likened it to a little girl who, wanting to be lifted, would say to her father, "Up, daddy. Up, daddy."[127]

Given Schaeffer's very strong emphasis on the power of prayer and on the importance of an experiential reality and the necessity of a relational understanding of God, it is difficult to see how critics like Clark Pinnock could accuse him of being a rationalist. Indeed one must question if they have really attempted to understand Schaeffer in the totality of his ministry and his writings. One often suspects that they take his three main apologetical books and study them in isolation from his other works and without reference to his spirituality. However, perhaps part of the fault is Schaeffer's. Some feel that his rationality and spirituality run like two parallel railroad tracks: going in the same direction but only running alongside each other and never meeting. There is a degree of truth in this in that Schaeffer never expressed a fully integrated view as to how his apologetics and spirituality united. Yet to be fair to him, he did say that one needed to consider his apologetics *and* the reality of the life of L'Abri "as the two sides of a single coin" to gain a proper understanding of his ministry.[128] Although he may never have presented a major theoretical overview explaining the integration of his rationality and spirituality, a practical demonstration was provided of the integration by the way he, Edith, their family, and subsequently other workers dealt with visitors to L'Abri.

As discussed in earlier sections, a genuine effort was made to welcome all individuals, and the attempts to build a sense of community and to show real compassion were costly and required sacrificial love. Indeed having watched the staff at different branches of L'Abri reach out to individuals, seek to provide answers to difficult questions, and cope with awkward (and sometimes just plain crooked) people, what struck me was the impossibility, humanly speaking, of doing so. Only a total reliance upon God and a willingness to minister in the power of the Holy Spirit made L'Abri possible. Having to share your home and life with spoiled college students from wealthy backgrounds while you, surviving on a very modest (and not even guaranteed) salary, struggle to provide for your own children is enough to embitter many a Christian worker. The fact that this has not become a major issue at L'Abri is testimony to the caliber of the workers, the sincerity of their spirituality, and the reality of the Holy Spirit. In mind-set and in everyday life the rationality and spirituality were united at L'Abri.

No Little People

When L'Abri started in 1955, it was a small and insignificant work, and there was no indication that it would grow or that the Schaeffers would gain the international recognition they later received. Indeed when Hurvey Woodson, who was to be the first worker at L'Abri alongside the Schaeffers, told friends he was going to Switzerland, he recalls that "everyone thought I was wasting my time because there really wasn't much of a work there."[129] Schaeffer was very content to accept that the work might remain very insignificant and often said that if the Lord called them to remain a very small work, they should accept it. This reflected his deeply held view that with God there are no little people and no little places, and the important thing for the Christian is to be what God wants you to be, where He wants you to be.[130] Schaeffer believed, and knew from personal experience, that "quietness and peace before God are more important than any influence a position may seem to give, for we must stay in step with God to have the power of the Holy Spirit."[131]

Although Schaeffer had no plans to develop the scale of the work, he always accepted that if God chose to extrude him (i.e., to force him under pressure) into a position of more responsibility and authority, he should be willing to accept that also. By the late 1970s Schaeffer was internationally renowned as a Christian apologist. He had written a number of books, several of which became immediate best-sellers (and Edith was well-known in her own right as a successful author). He had visited and lectured at the major universities in the UK and the USA.

He had made two major film series on key issues. He had become a major figure in the evangelical world and an outspoken critic of the secular world with access to senior politicians and public figures. Yet he continued to be interested in individuals and to give time to those whom others hardly noticed. Once while staying at a hotel in the United States when he was due to address a conference of several thousand people, he fell into conversation with the maid looking after the room. For Schaeffer, talking with one person was as important as talking to several thousand, and the social background of the person was irrelevant.

As his eldest daughter, Priscilla Sandri, observed of him, over the years in his conversations "he wasn't just trying to get people saved, he really had an emotional involvement."[132] This emotional involvement of his, his compassion for individuals, is in marked contrast to so many of the religious leaders and professionals we encounter. It is always revealing to watch such people "off-duty" and observe how they relate to those around them. When I attended a major international conference on apologetics, designed to enable Christians to reach out and relate more effectively with secular society, it was rather disappointing to see that many of the speakers and leading figures were not even aware of the hotel staff, never mind thanking them for their service or making an effort to reach them with the gospel.

Perhaps I am too hard on these people, perhaps I expect too much from them, and perhaps Francis Schaeffer is "the exception rather than the rule." When Os Guinness was asked to sum up his view of Schaeffer, he said, "At the heart of everything he did and behind the genius of his life, were three very simple things you don't often see in one person. A passionate love for God, a passionate love for people and a passionate love for truth." Noting that Edith shared this passion, Guinness added, "I have never seen this combined in any other couple I have ever met."[133] I strongly agree with this assessment by Guinness, and I believe it explains why the apologetics of Francis Schaeffer were so effective: people knew he cared, and they were willing to listen. As we seek to be authentic witnesses in our generation, let us listen to the words of Francis Schaeffer, and may we

Conclusion: Love as the Final Apologetic

remember throughout our lives that in God's sight there are no little people and no little places. Only one thing is important: to be consecrated persons in God's place for us, at each moment. Those who think of themselves as little people in little places, if committed to Christ and living under His Lordship in the whole of life, may, by God's grace, change the flow of our generation.[134]

NOTES

INTRODUCTION: SCHAEFFER IN CONTEXT

1. George M. Marsden, *Fundamentalism and American Culture: The Shaping of Twentieth-Century Evangelicalism, 1870–1925* (New York: Oxford University Press, 1980), p. 11.

2. Mark A. Noll, *A History of Christianity in the United States and Canada* (Grand Rapids, MI: Eerdmans, 1992), p. 364.

3. Nancy Pearcey, *Total Truth: Liberating Christianity from Its Cultural Captivity* (Wheaton, IL: Crossway Books, 2004), p. 155.

4. By "liberal" or "modernists" is meant that type of Christianity that emerged in response to, and in basic sympathy with, the Enlightenment. It maintains "that religious beliefs are fallible and are thus to be held tentatively." It holds that "theology should always interrelate the spirit of its own time and the Christian past in a manner that allows each to make an essential and substantive difference to the formulation of theological claims." Alister McGrath, ed., *The Blackwell Encyclopaedia of Modern Christian Thought* (Oxford: Basil Blackwell, 1993), p. 325.

5. Among the doctrines stressed by the fundamentalists were "an inspired and inerrant Bible; the deity of Christ and His atoning death for sin on the Cross; His bodily resurrection and ascension; and His return to judge the world, consign the Devil and unrepentant sinners to hell and resurrect those who belonged to Christ to live eternally in heaven with God." Ibid., p. 230.

6. Ibid., p. 189.

7. W. R. Godfrey, "The Westminster School," in David F. Wells, ed., *Reformed Theology in America* (Grand Rapids, MI: Eerdmans, 1985), p. 93.

8. D. G. Hart, *Defending the Faith: J. Gresham Machen and the Crisis of Conservative Protestantism* (Phillipsburg, NJ: P & R, 2003), pp. 151-154.

9. Ned B. Stonehouse, *J. Gresham Machen* (Edinburgh: Banner of Truth Trust, 1954, 1987), p. 501.

10. Godfrey, "The Westminster School," p. 93.

11. Hart, *Defending the Faith*, pp. 162-165.

12. Premillennial dispensationalism placed a strong emphasis on eschatology, and its inherent pessimism "could be seen as predicting the rise of modernism, secularism and apostate religious structures." McGrath, *The Blackwell Encyclopaedia of Modern Christian Thought*, p. 231.

13. Noll, *A History of Christianity in the United States and Canada*, p. 385.

14. D. G. Hart and Mark A. Noll, eds., *Dictionary of the Presbyterian and Reformed Tradition in America* (Downers Grove, IL: InterVarsity Press, 1999), p. 36.

15. Christopher Catherwood, *Five Evangelical Leaders* (London: Hodder & Stoughton, 1984), p. 112.

16. For details, see Edith Schaeffer, *The Tapestry: The Life and Times of Francis and Edith Schaeffer* (Nashville: Word, 1981), pp. 175-405.

17. Lane T. Dennis, ed., *The Letters of Francis Schaeffer* (Wheaton, IL: Crossway Books, 1985), letter dated April 14, 1951, p. 32.

18. Ibid., letter dated February 12, 1955, p. 52.

19. For details, see Edith Schaeffer, *L'Abri* (Wheaton, IL: Crossway Books, 1992), pp. 18-25, 63-111.

20. Ibid., p. 124.

21. Catherwood, *Five Evangelical Leaders*, p. 121.

22. Francis Schaeffer, *True Spirituality* (Wheaton, IL: Tyndale, 1971), p. x.

CHAPTER ONE: CALVIN AND THE REFORMED TRADITION

1. By *apologetics* is meant the reasoned defense of Christianity, which might "be expected to include argument to the effect (1) that there is a God; (2) that human beings are estranged from God; (3) that the life and death of Jesus Christ would be such as to constitute a remedy for this estrangement; and (4) that this life and death occurred as a matter of historical fact." Alister McGrath, ed., *The Blackwell Encyclopaedia of Modern Christian Thought* (Oxford: Basil Blackwell, 1993), p. 9.

2. W. Andrew Hoffecker and G. K. Beale, "Biblical Epistemology:

Revelation," in Andrew Hoffecker and Gary Scott Smith, eds., *Building a Christian World View* (Phillipsburg, NJ: P & R, 1986), p. 196. Religious epistemology is the branch of philosophy devoted to the question of how we know God and the justification of claims to religious knowledge. For further details see W. J. Wood, *Epistemology: Becoming Intellectually Virtuous* (Leicester: Apollos, 1998).

3. Ford Lewis Battles has shown how the great emphasis by the humanists on the Greek and Latin classics continued to be reflected in Calvin's writings, while his plans for the Geneva Academy involved a curriculum that meant an integration of the Reformed faith and study of the classical writers. Robert Benedetto, ed., *Interpreting John Calvin* (Grand Rapids, MI: Baker Books, 1996), pp. 62-65.

4. J. M. Houston, "Knowing God: The Transmission of Reformed Theology," in Donald M. Lewis and Alister McGrath, eds., *Doing Theology for the People of God* (Leicester: Apollos, 1996), p. 230.

5. W. A. Hoffecker, "Medieval Scholasticism: The Thomistic Synthesis," in ibid., p. 107. However, another Reformed scholar disputes this view of Aquinas and argues that Aquinas believed in the priority of revealed theology. For details, see Arvin Vos, *Aquinas, Calvin and Contemporary Protestant Thought* (Washington, DC: Christian University Press, 1985), pp. 94-95.

6. Alister McGrath, *The Intellectual Origins of the European Reformation* (Oxford: Basil Blackwell, 1987), p. 191.

7. Colin Brown, *Christianity and Western Thought* (Leicester: Apollos, 1990), pp. 153-154.

8. David Steinmetz, *Calvin in Context* (Oxford: Oxford University Press, 1995), p. 152.

9. McGrath, *The Intellectual Origins*, p. 57.

10. Steinmetz, *Calvin in Context*, p. 136.

11. John Calvin, *Institutes of the Christian Religion* (1559), trans. H. Beveridge (Grand Rapids, MI: Eerdmans, 1989), p. 43.

12. Charles Sherlock, *The Doctrine of Humanity* (Leicester: IVP, 1996), p. 78.

13. Calvin, *Institutes*, p. 55.

14. B. A. Gerrish, *The Old Protestantism and the New: Essays on the Reformation Heritage* (Chicago: The University of Chicago Press, 1982), p. 154.

15. Louis Berkhof, *Systematic Theology* (Edinburgh: Banner of Truth, 1939, 1958), p. 202.

16. Calvin, *Institutes*, p. 233.

17. Ibid., p. 237.

18. Edward A. Dowey, *The Knowledge of God in Calvin's Theology* (Grand Rapids, MI: Eerdmans, 1952, 1994), p. 22.

19. Calvin, *Institutes*, pp. 233, 238.

20. John Calvin, *The Epistle of Paul to the Romans* (1540), trans. D. W. Torrance (Grand Rapids, MI: Eerdmans, 1960), p. 31.

21. Ibid., p. 32.

22. J. Van Engen, "Natural Law," in Walter A. Elwell, ed., *Evangelical Dictionary of Theology* (Basingstoke: Marshall, Morgan and Scott, 1985), p. 751.

23. Calvin, *Institutes,* p. 64.

24. Susan E. Schreiner, *The Theater of His Glory: Nature and the Natural Order in the Thought of John Calvin* (Grand Rapids, MI: Baker, 1991), p. 72.

25. Calvin, *Institutes*, pp. 40, 455.

26. Ibid., p. 65.

27. Ibid., p. 83.

28. Ibid., pp. 76-82.

29. Ibid., p. 72.

30. Ibid., p. 84.

31. Schreiner, *The Theater of His Glory*, p. 72.

32. Ibid., p. 77.

33. Calvin, *The Epistle of Paul to the Romans*, p. 48.

34. Calvin, *Institutes*, pp. 38, 51.

35. Brown, *Christianity and Western Thought*, p. 153.

36. Schreiner, *The Theater of His Glory*, p. 66.

37. Dowey, *The Knowledge of God in Calvin's Theology*, p. 7.

38. Calvin, *Institutes*, p. 229.

39. Ibid., pp. 234-245.

40. Ibid., p. 236.

41. Henry R. Van Til, *The Calvinistic Concept of Culture* (Phillipsburg, NJ: P & R, 1959), p. 116.

42. McGrath, *Blackwell Encyclopaedia of Modern Christian Thought*, p. 400.

43. P. E. Hughes, "Grace," in Elwell, *Evangelical Dictionary of Theology*, p. 481.

44. Abraham Kuyper, "Common Grace," in J. D. Bratt, ed., *Abraham Kuyper: A Centennial Reader* (Grand Rapids, MI: Eerdmans, 1998), p. 175.

45. Ibid., p. 176.

46. Berkhof, *Systematic Theology*, p. 206.

47. "Christian Knowledge," in *Jonathan Edwards on Knowing Christ* (Edinburgh: Banner of Truth Trust, 1990), p. 17.

48. Ibid.

49. Ibid., p. 12.

50. Ibid., p. 13.

51. Ibid., p. 14.

52. Ibid., p. 13.

53. J. I. Packer, *Among God's Giants* (Eastbourne: Kingsway, 1991), p. 411.

54. "Christian Knowledge," pp. 13-14.

55. Ibid., p. 15.

56. C. Trueman, "On the Shoulders of Giants," in *Themelios*, Vol. 24, No. 2, February 1999, p. 1.

57. D. B. Calhoun, *Princeton Seminary: The Majestic Testimony, 1869–1929* (Edinburgh: Banner of Truth Trust, 1996), p. 182.

58. B. B. Warfield, *Calvin and Augustine* (Philadelphia: P & R, 1909, 1956), p. 37.

59. Ibid., p. 41.

60. Ibid., pp. 41-42.

61. Calhoun, *Princeton Seminary: The Majestic Testimony, 1869–1929*, p. 182.

62. Peter Hicks, *Evangelicals and Truth* (Leicester: IVP, 1998), p. 67.

63. Alister McGrath, *A Passion for Truth: The Intellectual Coherence of Evangelicalism* (Leicester: IVP, 1996), pp. 167-169.

64. Calhoun, *Princeton Seminary: The Majestic Testimony, 1869–1929*, p. 413.

65. Ibid.

66. R. J. Vander Molen, "Protestant Scholasticism," in Elwell, *Evangelical Dictionary of Theology*, p. 935.

67. George M. Marsden, "American Evangelical Academia," in Alvin Plantinga and Nicholas Wolterstorff, eds., *Faith and Rationality: Reason and Belief in God* (Notre Dame, IN: University of Notre Dame Press, 1983), p. 253.

68. W. R. Godfrey, "The Westminster School," in David F. Wells, ed., *Reformed Theology in America* (Grand Rapids, MI: Eerdmans, 1985), p. 97. This point appears to contradict Kuyper's doctrine of common grace, and it is one of the tensions in his writings that needs further consideration; but that is outside the scope of this book.

69. Marsden, "American Evangelical Academia," p. 249.

70. Abraham Kuyper, "The Blurring of the Boundaries," in Bratt, *Abraham Kuyper: A Centennial Reader*, p. 396.

71. Marsden, "American Evangelical Academia," p. 248.

72. For details of the influence of Dutch thinkers upon American Reformed theology, see David F. Wells, ed., *Dutch Reformed Theology* (Grand Rapids, MI: Baker, 1989), and G. Harinck and H. Krabendam, eds., *Sharing the Reformed Tradition: The Dutch-North American Exchange, 1846-1996* (Amsterdam: VU Unitgeveriji, 1996).

73. Cornelius Van Til, *The Defense of the Faith* (Phillipsburg, NJ: P & R, 1955, 1967), pp. 96-102.

74. Ibid., p. 100.

75. W. Edgar, "Two Christian Warriors: Cornelius Van Til and Francis Schaeffer Compared," *The Westminster Theological Journal*, Vol. 57, No. 1, Spring 1995, p. 64.

76. F. Baird, "Schaeffer's Intellectual Roots," in R. W. Ruegsegger, ed., *Reflections on Francis Schaeffer* (Grand Rapids, MI: Zondervan, 1986), p. 64.

77. J. Gresham Machen, *What Is Faith?* (London: Hodder & Stoughton, 1925), p. 18.

78. Scott R. Burson and Jerry L. Walls, *C. S. Lewis and Francis Schaeffer: Lessons for a New Century* (Downers Grove, IL: InterVarsity Press, 1998), p. 143.

79. Francis Schaeffer, *He Is There and He Is Not Silent* (Leicester: IVP, 1972, 1990), p. 275.

80. Burson and Walls, *C. S. Lewis and Francis Schaeffer*, p. 143.

81. Francis Schaeffer, *Escape from Reason* (Leicester: IVP, 1968, 1990), p. 207.

CHAPTER TWO: ARGUMENTS AND APPROACH

1. David Porter, "Francis Schaeffer," in John D. Woodbridge, ed., *Great Leaders of the Christian Church* (Chicago: Moody Press, 1988), p. 361.

2. J. I. Packer, "No Little Person," in R. W. Ruegsegger, ed., *Reflections on Francis Schaeffer* (Grand Rapids, MI: Zondervan, 1986), p. 8.

3. Francis A. Schaeffer, *The God Who Is There* (Leicester: IVP, 1968, 1990), p. 176.

4. Harold O. J. Brown, "Standing Against the World," in Lane T. Dennis, ed., *Francis A. Schaeffer: Portraits of the Man and His Work* (Wheaton, IL: Crossway Books, 1985), p. 16.

5. Schaeffer, *The God Who Is There*, p. 187.

6. Packer, "No Little Person," p. 11. The idea about the primacy of thought will be more fully considered in Chapter Three.

7. Schaeffer, *The God Who Is There*, p. 153.

8. Francis A. Schaeffer, *Two Contents: Two Realities* (London: Hodder & Stoughton, 1974), p. 10.

9. C. S. Lewis, "Christian Apologetics," in *Compelling Reason* (London: Fount Paperbacks, 1996), p. 76.

10. Schaeffer, *The God Who Is There*, p. 177.

11. Francis A. Schaeffer, *Death in the City* (Leicester: IVP, 1969, 1977), p. 77.

12. Francis A. Schaeffer, *Escape from Reason* (Leicester: IVP, 1968, 1990), pp. 269-270.

13. Schaeffer, *The God Who Is There*, p. 155.

14. Francis A. Schaeffer, *He Is There and He Is Not Silent* (Leicester: IVP, 1972, 1990), p. 275.

15. Schaeffer, *The God Who Is There*, p. 6.

16. Ibid., p. 8.

17. Ibid., p. 201.

18. Ibid., p. 6.

19. Ibid., p. 7.

20. Schaeffer, *Escape from Reason*, p. 211.

21. Ibid., p. 214.

22. Schaeffer, *He Is There and He Is Not Silent*, p. 306.

23. Schaeffer, *Escape from Reason*, p. 215.

24. Schaeffer, *He Is There and He Is Not Silent*, p. 307.

25. Schaeffer, *Escape from Reason*, p. 216.

26. Schaeffer, *He Is There and He Is Not Silent*, p. 307.

27. Schaeffer, *Escape from Reason*, p. 216.

28. Ibid., p. 228.

29. Ibid., p. 229.

30. Ibid., p. 230.

31. Ibid., p. 229.

32. Schaeffer, *The God Who Is There*, p. 9, and *Escape from Reason*, pp. 228-229.

33. Schaeffer, *The God Who Is There*, p. 10.

34. Ibid.

35. Ibid., p. 14.

36. Schaeffer, *Escape from Reason*, p. 233.

37. Ibid.
38. Schaeffer, *The God Who Is There*, p. 15.
39. Schaeffer, *Escape from Reason*, p. 238.
40. Schaeffer, *The God Who Is There*, p. 16.
41. Schaeffer, *Escape from Reason*, p. 238.
42. Ibid., p. 239.
43. Ibid.
44. Ibid., p. 242.
45. Ibid., p. 243.
46. Schaeffer, *The God Who Is There*, p. 55.
47. Schaeffer, *Escape from Reason*, p. 240.
48. Ibid., p. 241.
49. Ibid., p. 242.
50. Ibid., p. 235.
51. Ibid., p. 255.
52. Ibid., p. 235.
53. Schaeffer, *The God Who Is There*, p. 132.
54. Ibid., p. 137.
55. Lecture by Rev. Francis Schaeffer at L'Abri on "Apologetics," 1963, Farel House tape no. 73A.
56. Schaeffer, *The God Who Is There*, p. 138.
57. Ibid., p. 132.
58. Ibid., p. 134.
59. Ibid., p. 139.
60. Ibid., p. 140.
61. Ibid., p. 138.
62. Ibid., p. 140.
63. Ibid., p. 142.
64. Ibid., p. 144.
65. Ibid., p. 145.
66. Schaeffer, *He Is There and He Is Not Silent*, p. 283.
67. Ibid., p. 278.
68. Ibid., p. 286.
69. Ibid., p. 287.
70. Ibid.
71. Ibid., p. 292.
72. Ibid., p. 293.

73. Ibid., p. 297.

74. Ibid., p. 298.

75. Ibid., p. 301.

76. Ibid., p. 322.

77. Schaeffer defined epistemology as "the theory of the method or grounds of knowledge; or the theory of knowledge; or how we know we know; or how do we know." Lecture by Rev. Francis Schaeffer at English L'Abri in 1972 on "Modern Man and Epistemology," Farel House tape no. X8.

78. Schaeffer, *He Is There and He Is Not Silent*, p. 303.

79. Ibid., p. 324.

80. Ibid., p. 325.

81. Ibid., pp. 344-345.

82. Ibid., p. 345.

83. Schaeffer's understanding of inerrancy was similar to that of J. I. Packer who defined it as the conviction that the Bible in "all its teaching is the utterance of God who cannot lie, whose word once spoken, abides for ever, and that therefore it may be trusted implicitly." J. I. Packer, *"Fundamentalism" and the Word of God* (Grand Rapids, MI: Eerdmans, 1958), p. 95. For Schaeffer's own teaching on the importance of inerrancy see Francis A. Schaeffer, *No Final Conflict* (London: Hodder & Stoughton, 1975) and *The Great Evangelical Disaster* (Wheaton, IL: Crossway Books, 1984).

84. Schaeffer, *The God Who Is There*, p. 65.

85. Schaeffer, *He Is There and He Is Not Silent*, p. 334.

86. Ibid., p. 336.

87. Schaeffer, *The God Who Is There*, p. 145.

88. Ibid., p. 158.

89. Ibid., pp. 163-164.

90. Ibid., p. 176

91. Colin Duriez, "Francis Schaeffer," in Walter A. Elwell, ed., *Handbook of Evangelical Theologians* (Grand Rapids, MI: Baker Books, 1993), p. 251.

92. Lecture by Francis Schaeffer at L'Abri on "Apologetics," 1963, Farel House tape no. 73A.

93. Francis A. Schaeffer, *No Little People* (1974), in *The Complete Works of Francis A. Schaeffer* (Wheaton, IL: Crossway Books, 1982), Vol. 3, p. 13.

94. David Porter, "Francis Schaeffer," in John D. Woodbridge, ed., *Great Leaders of the Christian Church* (Chicago: Moody Press, 1988), p. 365.

95. Duriez, "Francis Schaeffer," p. 246.

96. Schaeffer, *The God Who Is There*, p. 130.

97. Schaeffer, *Escape from Reason*, p. 270.

98. Schaeffer, *He Is There and He Is Not Silent*, p. 285.

99. Schaeffer, *The God Who Is There*, p. 130.

100. Schaeffer, *Death in the City*, pp. 80-81.

101. Ibid., p. 81.

102. Schaeffer, *The God Who Is There*, p. 155.

103. Schaeffer, *Death in the City*, p. 61.

104. Ibid.

105. Schaeffer, *The God Who Is There*, p. 130.

106. Carl McIntire, in *The Christian Beacon*, Spring 1972, p. 3.

107. Lloyd-Jones had visited L'Abri as early as 1957 and had preached at the wedding of Schaeffer's eldest daughter, Priscilla, to John Sandri. Iain H. Murray, *D. Martyn Lloyd-Jones: The Fight of Faith* (Edinburgh: Banner of Truth Trust, 1990), p. 286.

108. D. Martyn Lloyd-Jones, *Preaching and Preachers* (London: Hodder & Stoughton, 1971, 1985), p. 49.

109. Ibid., pp. 50-51.

110. Ibid., p. 40.

111. In his final book, *The Great Evangelical Disaster* (Wheaton, IL: Crossway, 1984), published two months before he died, Schaeffer argued that inerrancy was a "watershed" issue for evangelicalism.

112. Edith Schaeffer, *L'Abri* (London: Hodder & Stoughton, 1969), pp. 31, 144-145.

113. In an interview with Barry Seagren at English L'Abri, June 17, 1999. Seagren first met Francis Schaeffer in 1965 and made his first visit to Swiss L'Abri in 1967. Marrying Veronica whom he met at L'Abri, they served at Swiss L'Abri until 1979. Moving to Southborough L'Abri, they worked at this branch until 1983 when they transferred to English L'Abri. They remained on its staff until 1992 when Barry became pastor of the International Presbyterian Church.

114. Schaeffer, *The God Who Is There*, p. 5.

115. Lecture by Francis Schaeffer at L'Abri in January 1964, "Basic Problem: Truth versus Contentless Experience," Farel House tape no. 43.4.

116. Ibid.

117. Schaeffer, *The God Who Is There*, p. 153.

118. Schaeffer, *Escape from Reason*, p. 269.
119. Lecture, "Basic Problem: Truth versus Contentless Experience."
120. Schaeffer, *Escape from Reason*, p. 270.
121. Lloyd-Jones, *Preaching and Preachers*, p. 51.
122. Schaeffer, *The God Who Is There*, p. 153.
123. Ibid., p. 185.
124. Ibid., p. 153.
125. Francis A. Schaeffer, *True Spirituality* (Wheaton, IL: Tyndale House, 1971), p. 57.
126. Schaeffer, *The God Who Is There*, p. 131.
127. Schaeffer, *Escape from Reason*, p. 367.
128. Lecture, "Basic Problem: Truth versus Contentless Experience."
129. Schaeffer, *The God Who Is There*, p. 185.
130. Ibid., p. 113.
131. Seagren interview.
132. Scott R. Burson and Jerry L. Walls, *C. S. Lewis and Francis Schaeffer: Lessons for a New Century* (Downers Grove, IL: InterVarsity Press, 1998), p. 72.
133. Ibid.
134. Schaeffer, *The God Who Is There*, p. 131.
135. Schaeffer, *No Little People*, p. 5.
136. Christopher Catherwood, *Five Evangelical Leaders* (London: Hodder & Stoughton, 1984), p. 139.
137. L. G. Parkhurst, *Francis Schaeffer: The Man and His Message* (Eastbourne: Kingsway Publications, 1986), p. 54.
138. Francis A. Schaeffer, *The Church at the End of the Twentieth Century* (London: Hodder & Stoughton, 1970, 1975), p. 132.
139. Schaeffer, *The God Who Is There*, p. 131.
140. Edith Schaeffer, *L'Abri*, p. 124.
141. Ibid., pp. 15-16.
142. Schaeffer, *True Spirituality*, p. ii.
143. Edith Schaeffer, *L'Abri*, p. 16.
144. Parkhurst, *Francis Schaeffer: The Man and His Message*, p. 85.
145. Burson and Walls, *C. S. Lewis and Francis Schaeffer: Lessons for a New Century*, p. 41.
146. Edith Schaeffer, *L'Abri*, p. 154.
147. Ibid., p. 139.

148. Ibid., p. 194.

149. Seagren interview.

150. Edith Schaeffer, *L'Abri*, p. 205.

151. Ibid.

152. Cited by Michael S. Hamilton, "The Dissatisfaction of Francis Schaeffer," *Christianity Today*, March 3, 1997.

153. Clark H. Pinnock, "Schaeffer on Modern Theology," in R. W. Ruegsegger, ed., *Reflections on Francis Schaeffer* (Grand Rapids, MI: Zondervan, 1986), pp. 173-174.

154. Seagren interview.

155. Edith Schaeffer, *L'Abri*, p. 123.

156. Catherwood, *Five Evangelical Leaders*, p. 137.

157. Ibid., p. 130.

158. Burson and Walls, *C. S. Lewis and Francis Schaeffer: Lessons for a New Century*, p. 151.

159. Seagren interview.

160. Quoted by Gavin McGrath in an interview on June 17, 1999. Author of *A Confident Life in an Age of Change*, McGrath served as a staff member at English L'Abri from 1995 until 1999.

161. J. B. Hurley, "Schaeffer on Evangelicalism" in Ruegsegger, *Reflections on Francis Schaeffer*, p. 276.

162. James W. Sire, in the Foreword to the 30th Anniversary Edition of *The God Who Is There* (Downers Grove, IL: InterVarsity Press, 1998), p. 17.

163. Catherwood, *Five Evangelical Leaders*, p. 130.

164. Address by Os Guinness at the memorial service for Francis Schaeffer in London in 1984, Farel House tape no. X656.

165. Francis A. Schaeffer, *The Mark of the Christian* (1970), in *The Complete Works of Francis A. Schaeffer* (Wheaton, IL: Crossway Books, 1982), Vol. 4, p. 199.

166. Schaeffer, *The Church at the End of the Twentieth Century*, p. 131.

167. Edith Schaeffer, *L'Abri*, 136.

168. Schaeffer, *The Church at the End of the Twentieth Century*, p. 129.

169. Ibid., p. 131.

170. Schaeffer, *Two Contents: Two Realities*, p. 29.

171. Ibid., p. 32.

172. Ibid., p. 33.

173. Schaeffer, *The Mark of the Christian*, p. 204.

174. Francis A. Schaeffer, *The Church Before the Watching World* (London: IVP, 1972), p. 53.
175. Ibid., p. 58.
176. Schaeffer, *The Church at the End of the Twentieth Century*, p. 170.
177. Burson and Walls, *C. S. Lewis and Francis Schaeffer: Lessons for a New Century*, p. 270.
178. M. Walford-Dellu, "You Can Have a Family with Us," in Dennis, *Francis A. Schaeffer: Portraits of the Man and His Work*, p. 137.
179. Pinnock, "Schaeffer on Modern Theology," p. 191.
180. Donald G. Bloesch, *Essentials of Evangelical Theology*, Vol. 2 (San Francisco: Harper & Row, 1979), p. 267.

CHAPTER THREE: RATIONALITY AND SPIRITUALITY

1. Alister McGrath, *A Passion for Truth: The Intellectual Coherence of Evangelicalism* (Leicester: Apollos, 1996), p. 170.
2. Van Til taught apologetics at Westminster Theological Seminary from its foundation in 1929 until his retirement in 1972. For a good insight into his thinking, see John M. Frame, *Cornelius Van Til: An Analysis of His Thought* (Phillipsburg, NJ: P & R, 1995).
3. William Edgar, "Two Christian Warriors: Cornelius Van Til and Francis Schaeffer Compared," in *The Westminster Theological Journal*, Vol. 57, No. 1, Spring 1995, p. 63.
4. Cornelius Van Til, *The Defense of the Faith* (Phillipsburg, NJ: Presbyterian and Reformed, 1955, 1967), p. 67.
5. J.M. Frame, "Cornelius Van Til," in Walter A. Elwell, ed., *Handbook of Evangelical Theologians* (Grand Rapids, MI: Baker Books, 1993), p. 163.
6. Ibid.
7. Edgar, "Two Christian Warriors: Cornelius Van Til and Francis Schaeffer Compared," p. 64.
8. Ibid.
9. Ibid., p. 65.
10. For further details, see ibid.
11. Cornelius Van Til, "The Apologetic Methodology of Francis A. Schaeffer," unpublished syllabus used at Westminster Theological Seminary, p. 26.

12. L. G. Parkhurst, *Francis Schaeffer: The Man and His Message* (Eastbourne: Kingsway, 1986), p. 81.

13. Even those who disagree with Van Til's approach acknowledge his dominant position within Reformed apologetics. For example, see John Gerstner, R. C. Sproul, and Arthur Lindsley, *Classical Apologetics* (Grand Rapids, MI: Zondervan, 1984), p. 183.

14. Steven B. Cowan, *Five Views on Apologetics* (Grand Rapids, MI: Zondervan, 2000), p. 19.

15. Francis A. Schaeffer, *The God Who Is There* (Leicester: IVP, 1968, 1990), p. 152.

16. Ibid., p. 153.

17. Ibid., p. 139.

18. Ibid., p. 138.

19. Scott R. Burson and Jerry L. Walls, *C. S. Lewis and Francis Schaeffer* (Downers Grove, IL: InterVarsity Press, 1998), p. 144.

20. Francis A. Schaeffer, "Presuppositionalism: A Review of a Review," *The Bible Today*, Vol. 42, No. 1, October 1948, p. 8.

21. Lecture by Francis Schaeffer at L'Abri in 1963 on "Apologetics," Farel House tape no. 73A.

22. Schaeffer, *The God Who Is There*, p. 132.

23. Lecture, "Apologetics."

24. Schaeffer, *The God Who Is There*, p. 138.

25. Ibid., p. 135.

26. Lecture, "Apologetics."

27. Ibid.

28. Schaeffer, *The God Who Is There*, p. 140.

29. Lecture, "Apologetics."

30. Schaeffer, *The God Who Is There*, p. 140.

31. Ibid., p. 142.

32. Ibid., p. 140.

33. Van Til, *The Defense of the Faith*, p. 82.

34. Ibid., p. 95.

35. Schaeffer, *The God Who Is There*, p. 138.

36. Lecture, "Apologetics."

37. Schaeffer, *The God Who Is There*, p. 137.

38. Lecture, "Apologetics."

39. Francis A. Schaeffer, *He Is There and He Is Not Silent* (Leicester: IVP, 1972, 1990), p. 278.

40. Francis A. Schaeffer, *Escape from Reason* (Leicester: IVP, 1969, 1990), p. 219.

41. Ibid., p. 267.

42. Schaeffer, *The God Who Is There*, p. 100.

43. Schaeffer, *He Is There and He Is Not Silent*, p. 340.

44. Schaeffer, *Escape from Reason*, p. 264.

45. Francis A. Schaeffer, *Back to Freedom and Dignity* (London: Hodder & Stoughton, 1973), p. 34.

46. Schaeffer, *He Is There and He Is Not Silent*, p. 278.

47. Schaeffer, *Escape from Reason*, p. 268.

48. Lecture by Francis Schaeffer at English L'Abri in 1974. "The Intellectual (Proof) and Faith," Farel House tape no. 8.1.

49. Schaeffer, *He Is There and He Is Not Silent*, p. 279.

50. Francis A. Schaeffer, *The New Super-Spirituality* (London: Hodder & Stoughton, 1973), p. 20.

51. Ibid., p. 21.

52. Schaeffer, *Escape from Reason*, p. 223.

53. Francis A. Schaeffer, *Two Contents: Two Realities* (London: Hodder & Stoughton, 1974), p. 10.

54. Francis A. Schaeffer, *Death in the City* (Leicester: IVP, 1969), p. 18.

55. Schaeffer, *The New Super-Spirituality*, p. 32.

56. Ibid.

57. Schaeffer, *The God Who Is There*, p. 123.

58. Ibid., p. 124.

59. Ibid., p. 153.

60. Ibid., p. 125.

61. Ibid., p. 133.

62. Ibid., p. 142.

63. In an interview with Ranald Macaulay on August 7, 1998. Macaulay first visited L'Abri in 1957, later married Schaeffer's second daughter, Susan, and served on the staff of L'Abri beginning in 1960. He and Susan founded and led English L'Abri until he returned to Swiss L'Abri in 1984 to serve as Director following the death of Francis Schaeffer.

64. Schaeffer, *The God Who Is There*, p. 145.

65. Schaeffer, *Escape from Reason*, p. 264.

66. Ibid.

67. Schaeffer, *The God Who Is There*, p. 101.

68. Schaeffer, *Escape from Reason*, p. 240.

69. Schaeffer, *The God Who Is There*, p. 145.

70. Schaeffer, *He Is There and He is Not Silent*, p. 289.

71. Ibid., p. 334.

72. For a sympathetic introduction to Barth's theology, see T. F. Torrance, *Karl Barth* (London: SCM Press, 1962).

73. Cornelius Van Til, *Christianity and Barthianism* (Phillipsburg, NJ: P & R, 1962, 1965), p. 315.

74. Lecture, "Apologetics." Comparing Van Til's approach to Barth's would be strongly contested by many scholars. This point will be considered in further detail in Chapter 4.

75. Schaeffer, *The God Who Is There*, p. 146.

76. Lecture, "Intellectual Proof and Faith."

77. Clark H. Pinnock, "Schaeffer on Modern Theology," in R. W. Ruegsegger, ed., *Reflections on Francis Schaeffer* (Grand Rapids, MI: Zondervan, 1986), p. 190.

78. Ibid., pp. 185, 188.

79. Ibid., p. 186.

80. Ibid., p. 187.

81. In Van Til, *Christianity and Barthianism*, p. 175.

82. Ibid., p. 311. A fuller study on the question as to whether Barth's theology changed in his later writings so much as to make him an ally of evangelical Christianity is outside the scope of this book. However, in passing I would just note that more recent research by Professor Bruce McCormack of Princeton Theological Seminary (published by Oxford University Press as *Karl Barth's Critically Realistic Dialectical Theology*) does not entirely agree with Van Til's interpretation of Barth. McCormack's magisterial study certainly deserves fuller attention. Yet, apart from McCormack, many of those seeking to interpret Barth in a new light are what might be termed "open" or "post-conservative" evangelicals. Despite their new interpretations, I am not aware of any of these writers whose work surpasses Van Til's *Christianity and Barthianism* in its thorough and comprehensive study of primary sources. Nor am I aware of any of these "open" evangelical writers who have engaged with Van Til's argument and established his assessment of Barth to be inaccu-

rate. I am therefore inclined to conclude that attempts to interpret Barth in a more sympathetic light reflect theological changes on the part of the "open" evangelical writers.

83. Pinnock, "Schaeffer on Modern Theology," p. 176.
84. Schaeffer, *Escape from Reason*, p. 219.
85. Schaeffer, *He Is There and He Is Not Silent*, p. 324.
86. Pinnock, "Schaeffer on Modern Theology," p. 177.
87. Schaeffer, *He Is There and He Is Not Silent*, p. 324.
88. Gordon H. Clark, *A Christian View of Men and Things* (Jefferson, MD: Trinity Foundation, 1952, 1991), p. 31.
89. David K. Clark, *Dialogical Apologetics* (Grand Rapids, MI: Baker Books, 1999), p. 48.
90. For example, see ibid. For those interested in an overview of Clark's epistemology, see Ronald Nash, "Gordon Clark's Theory of Knowledge," in Ronald Nash, ed., *The Philosophy of Gordon H. Clark: A Festschrift* (Phillipsburg, NJ: P & R, 1968), pp. 125-175.
91. Schaeffer, *The God Who Is There*, p. 121.
92. Schaeffer, *He Is There and He Is Not Silent*, p. 325.
93. David K. Clark, *Dialogical Apologetics*, p. 47.
94. Schaeffer, *He Is There and He Is Not Silent*, p. 336.
95. It was also alien to a large segment of Reformed theologians who took what the Schaeffers regarded to be a determinist view of God's sovereignty. See Edith Schaeffer, *The Tapestry* (Nashville: Word, 1981), pp. 189-190.
96. Schaeffer, *The God Who Is There*, p. 184.
97. Ibid., p. 112.
98. Ibid.
99. Schaeffer, *He Is There and He Is Not Silent*, p. 315.
100. Ibid., p. 316.
101. For example, see lectures by Francis Schaeffer at L'Abri on "Epistemology—the early Wittgenstein," Farel House tape nos. 11.2a and 11.2b.
102. Schaeffer, *The God Who Is There*, p. 184.
103. In an interview with Gavin McGrath on June 17, 1999. Author of *A Confident Life in an Age of Change* (Leicester: IVP, 1995), he served as a staff member at English L'Abri from 1995 until 1999.
104. Pinnock, "Schaeffer on Modern Theology," p. 178.

105. Schaeffer, *The God Who Is There*, p. 15.
106. Richard V. Pierard, "Schaeffer on History," in Ruegsegger, *Reflections on Francis Schaeffer*, p. 207.
107. Ibid., p. 209.
108. Ibid.
109. J. E. McGoldrick, *Abraham Kuyper: God's Renaissance Man* (Darlington, UK: Evangelical Press, 2000), p. 143.
110. David W. Bebbington, *Patterns in History: A Christian Perspective on Historical Thought* (Leicester: IVP, 1979, 1990), p. 137.
111. Harold O. J. Brown, "Standing Against the World," in Lane T. Dennis, ed., *Francis Schaeffer: Portraits of the Man and His Work* (Wheaton, IL: Crossway Books, 1986), p. 25.
112. For further details about idealism, see Colin Brown, *Philosophy and the Christian Faith* (London: Tyndale Press, 1969), pp. 117-124.
113. John M. Frame, "Cornelius Van Til," in Walter A. Elwell, ed., *Handbook of Evangelical Theologians* (Grand Rapids, MI: Baker Books, 1993), p. 157.
114. Pierard, "Schaeffer on History," p. 210.
115. Schaeffer, *The New Super-Spirituality*, pp. 8-18.
116. Francis A. Schaeffer, *How Should We Then Live?*, in *The Complete Works of Francis A. Schaeffer*, Vol. 5 (Wheaton, IL: Crossway Books, 1982, 1993), p. 230.
117. Lane T. Dennis, ed., *The Letters of Francis Schaeffer* (Eastbourne: Kingsway, 1986), letter dated July 19, 1963, p. 96.
118. Schaeffer, *Death in the City*, p. 92.
119. Ibid., p. 93.
120. Schaeffer, *How Should We Then Live?*, pp. 83-84.
121. Thomas V. Morris, *Francis Schaeffer's Apologetics: A Critique* (Chicago: Moody Press, 1976; later: Grand Rapids, MI: Baker Books, 1987), p. 78.
122. Ibid., p. 83.
123. Ibid., p. 79.
124. Gordon R. Lewis, "Schaeffer's Apologetic Method," in Ruegsegger, *Reflections on Francis Schaeffer*, p. 89.
125. Schaeffer, *The God Who Is There*, p. 130.
126. Ibid., p. 131.
127. Ibid., p. 176.
128. Lewis, "Schaeffer's Apologetic Method," p. 89.

129. E. R. Geehan, "The 'Presuppositional' Apologetics of Francis Schaeffer," *Themelios*, Vol. 8, No. 1, 1972, p. 17.
130. Schaeffer, *Escape from Reason*, p. 270.
131. Schaeffer, *The God Who Is There*, p. 130.
132. Schaeffer, *He Is There and He Is Not Silent*, p. 350.
133. Schaeffer, *The God Who Is There*, p. 142.
134. T. A. Noble, "Scripture and Experience," *Themelios*, Vol. 23, No. 1, October 1997, pp. 30-31.
135. Schaeffer, *The God Who Is There*, p. 65.
136. Ibid., p. 154.
137. Sermon by Francis Schaeffer at L'Abri on Romans 5:1-10, Farel House tape no. 1K.
138. Francis A. Schaeffer, *The Finished Work of Christ* (Leicester: IVP, 1998), pp. 124-125. Published posthumously, this book is based upon a series of Bible studies on the Epistle to the Romans that Francis Schaeffer conducted in 1960.
139. Interview with Barry Seagren at English L'Abri, June 17, 1999. Seagren first visited L'Abri in Switzerland in 1967 and then joined the staff there in 1969. He served there until 1979 when he moved to the Southborough branch and then switched to English L'Abri in 1983. He remained on its staff until 1992 when he became pastor of the local International Presbyterian church planted by L'Abri.
140. Ibid.
141. W. Rietkerk, *If Only I Could Believe!* (Carlisle, UK: Solway, 1997), p. xv.
142. Schaeffer, *The Finished Work of Christ*, p. 123.
143. Seagren interview.
144. Burson and Walls, *C. S. Lewis and Francis Schaeffer*, p. 54.
145. Lecture, "Apologetics."
146. "Presuppositionalism: A Review of a Review."
147. L. G. Parkhurst, "The Quiet Assurance of Truth," in Dennis, *Francis Schaeffer: Portraits of the Man and His Work*, p. 146.
148. McGrath interview.
149. Nicholas Wolterstorff, "Can Belief in God Be Rational If It Has No Foundations?" in Alvin Plantinga and Nicholas Wolterstorff, eds., *Faith and Rationality: Reason and Belief in God* (Notre Dame, IN: University of Notre Dame Press, 1983), p. 135.
150. Pinnock, "Schaeffer on Modern Theology," p. 174.

151. Seagren interview.

152. Schaeffer, *The God Who Is There*, pp. 164-165.

153. Ibid., p. 167.

154. Ibid., p. 185.

155. Ibid., p. 93.

156. Schaeffer, *The New Super-Spirituality*, p. 41.

157. Schaeffer, *The God Who Is There*, pp. 168-169.

158. Schaeffer, *Two Contents: Two Realities*, p. 25.

159. Seagren interview.

160. Schaeffer, *Two Contents: Two Realities*, pp. 9, 11, 25.

161. Francis A. Schaeffer, *True Spirituality* (Wheaton, IL: Tyndale, 1971), p. 55.

162. Schaeffer, *The New Super-Spirituality*, p. 43.

163. Schaeffer, *True Spirituality*, p. 70.

164. Ibid., p. 74.

165. Ibid., p. 72.

166. Ibid., p. 60.

167. Ibid.

168. Ibid., p. 64.

169. Ibid., p. 84.

170. Ibid., p. 79.

171. Ibid., p. 106.

172. Ibid., p. x.

173. Dennis, *Letters of Francis Schaeffer*, letter dated October 26, 1951, p. 36.

174. Pinnock, "Schaeffer on Modern Theology," p. 191.

175. Schaeffer, *The God Who Is There*, p. 157.

176. Ibid.

177. Burson and Walls, *C. S. Lewis and Francis Schaeffer*, p. 58.

178. Ibid., p. 62.

179. Schaeffer, *The Finished Work of Christ*, p. 118.

180. Schaeffer, *True Spirituality*, p. 148.

181. Schaeffer, *The Finished Work of Christ*, p. 121.

182. Schaeffer, *The God Who Is There*, p. 172.

183. Dennis, *Letters of Francis Schaeffer*, letter dated November 12, 1954, p. 49.

184. Schaeffer, *The Finished Work of Christ*, p. 125.

185. Schaeffer, *The God Who Is There*, p. 173.

186. Edith Schaeffer, *L'Abri* (London: Hodder & Stoughton, 1969), p. i.

187. Schaeffer, *The New Super-Spirituality*, p. 44.
188. Sermon by Francis Schaeffer on "Prayer," 1964, Farel House tape no. 24.2.
189. Ibid.
190. Second sermon by Francis Schaeffer on "Prayer," 1964, Farel House tape no. 24.3.
191. First sermon on prayer; see note 188.
192. Ibid.
193. The doctrine of total depravity does not imply that every person is as thoroughly depraved as he can be, but that the corruption of sin extends to every aspect of his nature. Louis Berkhof, *Systematic Theology* (Edinburgh: Banner of Truth Trust, 1939, 1958), p. 247.
194. Schaeffer, *The God Who Is There*, p. 120.
195. Lecture, "Apologetics."
196. Lecture by Francis Schaeffer at L'Abri in January 1964 on "Basic Problem: Truth versus Contentless Experience," Farel House tape no. 43.4.
197. Seagren interview.
198. In an interview with Jerram Barrs on August 7, 1998. Barrs served at Swiss and English L'Abri before taking up the position of Professor of Contemporary Culture at the Francis Schaeffer Institute, Covenant Theological Seminary.
199. Schaeffer, *The Finished Work of Christ*, pp. 31-32.
200. Ibid., p. 33.
201. Macaulay interview.
202. McGrath interview.
203. Lecture by Ranald Macaulay on "The Christian Mind," at a L'Abri Conference, Farel House tape no. 156.3.
204. George Marsden, "American Evangelical Academia," in Plantinga and Wolterstorff, *Faith and Rationality: Reason and Belief in God*, p. 251.
205. Geehan, "The 'Presuppositional' Apologetics of Francis Schaeffer," p. 17.
206. Lewis, "Schaeffer's Apologetic Method," p. 95.
207. Copy of an unpublished letter from Francis Schaeffer, June 29, 1981, which was in the possession of Jim Ingram while serving as Director of Swiss L'Abri.
208. Ibid.
209. Ibid.

CHAPTER FOUR: ACADEMIC OR APOLOGIST?

1. Scott R. Burson and Jerry L. Walls, *C. S. Lewis and Francis Schaeffer: Lessons for a New Century from the Most Influential Apologists of Our Time* (Downers Grove, IL: InterVarsity, 1998), p. 143.

2. Francis A. Schaeffer, *The God Who Is There* (Leicester: IVP, 1968, 1990), p. 176.

3. Thomas V. Morris, *Francis Schaeffer's Apologetics: A Critique* (Chicago: Moody Press, 1976; later: Grand Rapids, MI: Baker Books, 1987), pp. 17, 20.

4. Ibid., p. 22.

5. Ibid., p. 23. It should be noted that Morris acknowledges that he is "borrowing the term 'argument from design' and using it loosely, not in its traditional, specifically teleological sense." Ibid., p. 22.

6. Francis A. Schaeffer, *He Is There and He Is Not Silent* (Leicester: IVP, 1972, 1990), p. 277.

7. Morris, *Francis Schaeffer's Apologetics: A Critique*, p. 32.

8. Ibid., p. 33.

9. Ibid., p. 35.

10. Ibid., p. 56.

11. Ibid., p. 57.

12. Ibid., p. 60.

13. Ibid., pp. 63-64.

14. Ibid., p. 58.

15. Ibid.

16. Ibid., p. 61.

17. See, for example, R. W. Ruegsegger, "Francis Schaeffer on Philosophy," in R. W. Ruegsegger, ed., *Reflections on Francis Schaeffer* (Grand Rapids, MI: Zondervan, 1986), pp. 107-130.

18. Richard V. Pierard, "Schaeffer on History," in Ruegsegger, ibid., pp. 208, 212.

19. Morris, *Francis Schaeffer's Apologetics: A Critique*, p. 66.

20. Ibid., p. 67.

21. Ibid., p. 70.

22. Ibid., p. 73.

23. Forrest Baird, "Schaeffer's Intellectual Roots," in Ruegsegger, *Reflections on Francis Schaeffer*, p. 64, and P. Hicks, *Evangelicals and Truth* (Leicester: IVP, 1998), p. 103.

24. Gordon R. Lewis, "Schaeffer's Apologetic Method," in Ruegsegger, *Reflections on Francis Schaeffer*, p. 89.

25. Kelly James Clark, *Return to Reason: A Critique of Enlightenment Evidentialism* (Grand Rapids, MI: Eerdmans, 1998), p. 3.

26. David K. Clark, *Dialogical Apologetics: A Person-Centered Approach to Christian Defense* (Grand Rapids, MI: Baker Books, 1993), p. 34.

27. Ibid., p. 36.

28. Ibid., p. 39

29. Clark, *Return to Reason: A Critique of Enlightenment Evidentialism*, p. 138.

30. Alvin Plantinga, "Reason and Belief in God," in Alvin Plantinga and Nicholas Wolterstorff, eds., *Faith and Rationality: Reason and Belief in God* (Notre Dame, IN: University of Notre Dame Press, 1983), p. 62.

31. Nicholas Wolterstorff, "Can Belief in God Be Rational?" in ibid., p. 137.

32. Ibid., p. 65.

33. Clark, *Return to Reason: A Critique of Enlightenment Evidentialism*, p. 43.

34. For details of how Reformed epistemologists understand a belief is warranted and how they explain the work of the Holy Spirit, see C. Stephen Evans, *The Historical Christ and the Jesus of Faith: The Incarnational Narrative as History* (Oxford: Oxford University Press, 1996), pp. 260-281.

35. Ibid., p. 264.

36. Ibid., p. 271.

37. George M. Marsden, *Fundamentalism and American Culture* (New York: Oxford University Press, 1980), p. 216.

38. J. Gresham Machen, *Christianity and Liberalism* (Grand Rapids, MI: Eerdmans, 1923, 1992), pp. 20-22.

39. Lewis, "Schaeffer's Apologetic Method," p. 73.

40. D. B. Calhoun, *Princeton Seminary: The Majestic Testimony, 1869–1929*, Vol. II (Edinburgh: Banner of Truth Trust, 1996), p. 20.

41. Mark A. Noll, *The Princeton Theology, 1812–1921* (Phillipsburg, NJ: P & R, 1983), p. 44.

42. Marsden, *Fundamentalism and American Culture*, p. 16.

43. George Marsden, "American Evangelical Academia," in Plantinga and Wolterstorff, *Faith and Rationality: Reason and Belief in God*, p. 248.

44. G. L. Bahnsen, "The Apologetical Tradition of the OPC," in Charles G. Dennison and Richard C. Gamble, eds., *Pressing Toward the Mark* (Philadelphia: Orthodox Presbyterian Church, 1986), p. 273.

45. John M. Frame, *Cornelius Van Til: An Analysis of His Thought* (Phillipsburg, NJ: P & R, 1995), p. 137.

46. John M. Frame, "Cornelius Van Til," in Walter A. Elwell, ed., *Handbook of Evangelical Theologians* (Grand Rapids, MI: Baker Books, 1993), p. 163.

47. Clark Pinnock, "Schaeffer on Modern Theology," in Ruegsegger, *Reflections on Francis Schaeffer*, p. 190.

48. Schaeffer, *The God Who Is There*, p. 7.

49. Ibid., p. 138.

50. Lecture by Francis Schaeffer at L'Abri in 1963 on "Apologetics," Farel House tape no. 73A.

51. Schaeffer, *The God Who Is There*, p. 7.

52. Ibid., p. 137.

53. Schaeffer may have been reluctant to name Van Til in case their difference became a public personalized dispute. Since his spiritual crisis in 1951, Schaeffer believed that personal attacks on other Christians were "completely ruinous spiritually." Lane T. Dennis, ed., *The Letters of Francis Schaeffer* (Eastbourne: Kingsway, 1985), p. 67, letter dated August 29, 1956.

54. Lecture, "Apologetics."

55. Ibid.

56. William Edgar, "Two Christian Warriors: Cornelius Van Til and Francis Schaeffer Compared," in *The Westminster Theological Journal*, Vol. 57, No. 1, Spring 1995, p. 65.

57. Schaeffer, *The God Who Is There*, p. 152.

58. Ibid., p. 201.

59. Francis A. Schaeffer, *The God Who Is There* (London: Hodder & Stoughton, 1965, 1970), p. 14.

60. Interestingly, though Van Til is seen as the father of presuppositionalism, he used the word *presuppositionalist* rather sparingly, and he never really defined the term *presupposition*. Frame, *Cornelius Van Til: An Analysis of His Thought*, pp. 131-117.

61. Schaeffer, *He Is There and He Is Not Silent*, p. 324.

62. Interview with Jerram Barrs at Cambridge, August 7, 1998.

63. Interview with Barry Seagren at English L'Abri, June 17, 1999.

64. Burson and Walls, *C. S. Lewis and Francis Schaeffer: Lessons for a New Century from the Most Influential Apologists of Our Time*, p. 148.

65. Cornelius Van Til, "The Apologetic Methodology of Francis A.

Schaeffer," unpublished syllabus used at Westminster Theological Seminary, p. 50.

66. Ibid., p. 53.
67. Ibid., p. 3.
68. Ibid., p. 8.
69. Ibid., p. 11.
70. Ibid., p. 13.
71. Ibid., p. 50.
72. Ibid., p. 16.
73. Ibid., p. 8.
74. Ibid., p. i.
75. Ibid., p. 49.
76. Burson and Walls, *C. S. Lewis and Francis Schaeffer: Lessons for a New Century from the Most Influential Apologists of Our Time*, pp. 146-148.
77. Schaeffer, *The God Who Is There*, 1970 edition, p. 14.
78. Hicks, *Evangelicals and Truth*, p. 106.
79. Lewis, "Schaeffer's Apologetic Method," p. 79.
80. Colin Brown, *Philosophy and the Christian Faith* (London: Tyndale Press, 1969), p. 265.
81. Ibid.
82. Lewis, "Schaeffer's Apologetic Method," p. 88.
83. David K. Clark, *Return to Reason: A Critique of Enlightenment Evidentialism*, p. 105.
84. Lewis, "Schaeffer's Apologetic Method," p. 71.
85. Edward John Carnell (1919–1967) taught at Fuller Theological Seminary from 1948 until his death, serving as its president for five years. Among his many publications was the prize-winning *An Introduction to Christian Apologetics*, which established him as a serious scholar among American evangelicals. For further details see Rudolph Nelson, *The Making and Unmaking of an Evangelical Mind: The Case of Edward Carnell* (New York: Cambridge University Press, 1987), and Gordon R. Lewis, "Edward John Carnell," in Elwell, *Handbook of Evangelical Theologians*.
86. Edward J. Carnell, *An Introduction to Christian Apologetics* (Grand Rapids, MI: Eerdmans, 1948, 1981), p. 11.
87. Ibid., p. 56.
88. Ibid., p. 58.
89. Ibid., p. 163.

90. Ibid., p. 164.
91. Ibid., p. 8.
92. Ibid., p. 157.
93. Ibid., pp. 91-92.
94. Ibid., p. 92.
95. Ibid., p. 94.
96. Ibid., p. 115.
97. Ibid., p. 215.
98. Ibid., p. 222.
99. Ibid., p. 8.
100. Ibid., p. 219.
101. For details, see Lewis, "Schaeffer's Apologetic Method," pp. 77-86.
102. Edward J. Carnell, *Christian Commitment: An Apologetic* (New York: Macmillan, 1957), pp. 73-76.
103. E. R. Geehan, "The 'Presuppositional' Apologetic of Francis Schaeffer," in *Themelios*, Vol. 8, No. 1, 1972, p. 18.
104. Van Til, "The Apologetic Methodology of Francis A. Schaeffer," p. 50.
105. Ibid., Preface.
106. Francis A. Schaeffer, "Presuppositionalism: A Review of a Review," *The Bible Today*, Vol. 42, No. 1, October 1948, p. 9.]
107. Frame, *Cornelius Van Til: An Analysis of His Thought*, p. 294.
108. At a meeting with Karl Barth in 1962, Carnell was perceived to identify with Barth and was attacked for failing to challenge him. Apart from the dispute over his views on biblical inerrancy, Carnell's death in 1967 (from an overdose of drugs while suffering depression and insomnia) was controversial. Gordon R. Lewis, "Edward John Carnell," in Elwell, *Handbook of Evangelical Theologians*, pp. 330, 332.
109. Carnell, *Christian Commitment*, p. vii.
110. Schaeffer, *The God Who Is There*, p. 186.
111. Schaeffer, *He Is There and He Is Not Silent*, p. 303.
112. Ibid., p. 316.
113. Schaeffer, *The God Who Is There*, p. 23.
114. Ibid., p. 123.
115. Lecture by Francis Schaeffer at L'Abri in 1963 on "Apologetics," Farel House tape no. 73A.
116. Schaeffer, *The God Who Is There*, p. 178.

117. Burson and Walls, *C. S. Lewis and Francis Schaeffer: Lessons for a New Century from the Most Influential Apologists of Our Time*, p. 249.

118. Ibid., p. 237.

119. Brown, *Philosophy and the Christian Faith*, p. 264.

120. *Christianity Today*, March 3, 1997, p. 6.

121. Pinnock, "Schaeffer on Modern Theology," p. 185.

122. Ibid., p. 188.

123. Box cover of the Video Curriculum Kit for *Whatever Happened to the Human Race?*, Gospel Films, Muskegon, MI.

124. James I. Packer, "No Little Person," in Ruegsegger, *Reflections on Francis Schaeffer*, p. 15.

125. Edith Schaeffer, *L'Abri* (Wheaton, IL: Crossway Books, 1969, 1992), pp. 124-125.

126. Franky approached his father about making the two film series and badgered him into doing so without delay or further reflection. The budget for the first film series (*How Should We Then Live?*) exceeded one million dollars. For an insight into the impulsive activism of Franky Schaeffer, see Edith Schaeffer, *The Tapestry* (Nashville: Word Books, 1981), pp. 577, 600-601.

127. The commercialism associated with the film series upset a number of long-serving L'Abri workers. See Christopher Catherwood, "Francis Schaeffer," in *Five Evangelical Leaders* (London: Hodder & Stoughton, 1984), pp. 147-148.

128. Franky's writings reveal a certain sarcastic attitude and lack a mature Christian relational dimension. For example, in the 1980s he wrote several books attacking the "pathetic servility" of prominent evangelicals. After he left evangelicalism for Eastern Orthodoxy he wrote a novel, which was widely perceived as drawing on his own family experiences and can only be described as cruel.

129. Pinnock, "Schaeffer on Modern Theology," p. 185.

130. Clark Pinnock, "Schaefferism as a World View," *Sojourners*, 6, No. 8 (July 1977), p. 33.

131. This was stated in private as well as in large public meetings. Baird, "Schaeffer's Intellectual Roots," p. 64.

132. Brown, *Philosophy and the Christian Faith*, p. 265.

133. Burson and Walls, *C. S. Lewis and Francis Schaeffer: Lessons for a New Century from the Most Influential Apologists of Our Time*, p. 240.

134. Schaeffer, *The God Who Is There*, p. 186.

135. Francis A. Schaeffer, *The Finished Work of Christ: Themes from Romans* (Leicester: IVP, 1998), pp. 118-119.

136. Schaeffer, *The God Who Is There*, p. 186.

137. L. G. Parkhurst, "The Quiet Assurance of Truth," in Lane T. Dennis, ed., *Francis A. Schaeffer: Portraits of the Man and His Work* (Wheaton, IL: Crossway Books, 1986), p. 145.

138. Schaeffer, *The God Who Is There*, p. 135.

139. In an interview with Barry Seagren on June 17, 1999 at English L'Abri.

140. Schaeffer, *The God Who Is There*, p. 131.

141. M. Walford-Dellu, "You Can Have a Family with Us," in Dennis, *Francis Schaeffer: Portraits of the Man and His Work*, p. 136.

142. Michael Hamilton, "The Dissatisfaction of Francis Schaeffer," *Christianity Today*, March 3, 1997, p. 30.

143. Lecture by Francis A. Schaeffer, "Basic Problem: Truth versus Contentless Experience." Delivered at Swiss L'Abri in January 1964, Farel House tape library reference no. 43.4.

144. Hamilton, "The Dissatisfaction of Francis Schaeffer."

145. Francis A. Schaeffer, *The Church Before the Watching World* (London: IVP, 1972), p. 58.

146. Francis A. Schaeffer, *The Church at the End of the Twentieth Century* (London: Hodder & Stoughton, 1970), p. 169.

147. Francis A. Schaeffer, *Death in the City* (Leicester: IVP, 1969), p. 7.

148. Walford-Dellu, "You Can Have a Family with Us," p. 134.

149. Schaeffer, *The Church at the End of the Twentieth Century*, p. 131.

150. Burson and Walls, *C. S. Lewis and Francis Schaeffer: Lessons for a New Century from the Most Influential Apologists of Our Time*, p. 262.

CONCLUSION: LOVE AS THE FINAL APOLOGETIC

1. J. I. Packer, "No Little Person," in R. W. Ruegsegger, ed., *Reflections on Francis Schaeffer* (Grand Rapids, MI: Zondervan, 1986), p. 16.

2. For further details on the development of postmodernism, from a Christian perspective, see David Dockery, ed., *The Challenge of Postmodernism* (Grand Rapids, MI: Baker Books, 1997); Dennis McCallum, ed., *The Death of Truth* (Minneapolis: Bethany, 1996); Douglas Groothuis, *Truth Decay* (Leicester: IVP, 2000); and Gene E. Veith, *Guide to Contemporary Culture* (Leicester: Crossway Books, 1994).

3. D. A. Carson, *The Gagging of God: Christianity Confronts Pluralism* (Leicester: IVP Apollos, 1996), p. 10.

4. Alister McGrath, *A Passion for Truth* (Leicester: IVP Apollos, 1996), p. 177.

5. Ibid., p. 175.

6. Ibid., p. 200.

7. Dave Tomlinson, *The Post-Evangelical* (London: Triangle Books, 1995), pp. 196-197.

8. Alister McGrath, "Prophets of Doubt," *Alpha*, August 1996.

9. See my forthcoming publication, *Whatever Happened to the Truth* (Belfast: Titus Press).

10. Stanley Grenz, *A Primer on Postmodernism* (Grand Rapids, MI: Eerdmans, 1996), p. 162.

11. Michael Foucault, "Strategies of Power," in W. T. Anderson, ed., *The Truth About Truth: De-confusing and Re-constructing the Postmodern World* (New York: Putnam's Sons, 1995), p. 45.

12. Grenz, *A Primer on Postmodernism*, p. 165.

13. Douglas Groothuis, *Truth Decay: Defending Christianity Against the Challenges of Postmodernism*, p. 38.

14. Ibid.

15. Ibid., p. 40.

16. Francis Schaeffer, *Escape from Reason* (Leicester: IVP, 1968, 1990), p. 254.

17. Groothuis, *Truth Decay: Defending Christianity Against the Challenges of Postmodernism*, p. 41.

18. Carson, *The Gagging of God: Christianity Confronts Pluralism*, p. 10.

19. Millard J. Erickson, *Postmodernizing the Faith* (Grand Rapids, MI: Baker Books, 1998), p. 40.

20. Lane T. Dennis, ed., *The Letters of Francis Schaeffer* (Eastbourne: Kingsway, 1986), letter dated February 2, 1953, p. 42.

21. Scott R. Burson and Jerry L. Walls, *C. S. Lewis and Francis Schaeffer: Lessons for a New Century from the Most Influential Apologists of Our Time* (Downers Grove, IL: InterVarsity Press, 1998), p. 268.

22. Francis Schaeffer, *Death in the City* (Leicester: IVP, 1969), p. 54.

23. Ibid., p. 62.

24. Ibid.

25. Harold O. J. Brown, "Standing Against the World," in Lane T. Dennis, ed., *Francis Schaeffer: Portrait of the Man and His Work* (Wheaton, IL: Crossway Books, 1986), p. 26.

26. Burson and Walls, *C. S. Lewis and Francis Schaeffer: Lessons for a New Century from the Most Influential Apologists of Our Time*, p. 269.

27. Christopher Catherwood, *Five Evangelical Leaders* (London: Hodder & Stoughton, 1984), p. 139.

28. Sylvester Jacobs, interviewed on "L'Abri: Truth and Love," Part II of "The Story of Francis and Edith Schaeffer," produced by RBC Ministries for *Day of Discovery*, USA, 2003.

29. Catherwood, *Five Evangelical Leaders*, p. 130.

30. Francis Schaeffer, *The Church at the End of the Twentieth Century* (London: Hodder & Stoughton, 1970), p. 189.

31. Francis A. Schaeffer, *The Church Before the Watching World* (Leicester: IVP, 1972), p. 67.

32. Edith Schaeffer, *The Tapestry: The Life and Times of Francis and Edith Schaeffer* (Nashville: Word Books, 1981), p. 223.

33. Francis A. Schaeffer, *Two Contents: Two Realities* (London: Hodder & Stoughton, 1974), p. 21.

34. Ibid., p. 22.

35. Interview with Barry Seagren, June 17, 1999, who said that following the publication of Schaeffer's first books in 1968, numbers increased dramatically, and L'Abri was thereafter busy throughout the year and not only during the summer season.

36. Kelly Monroe, "Finding God at Harvard," in D. A. Carson, ed., *Telling the Truth: Evangelizing Postmoderns* (Grand Rapids, MI: Zondervan, 2000), pp. 303-305.

37. Os Guinness, interviewed on "L'Abri: Truth and Love," Part II of "The Story of Francis and Edith Schaeffer," produced by RBC Ministries for *Day of Discovery*, USA, 2003.

38. Carson, *The Gagging of God: Christianity Confronts Pluralism*, p. 32.

39. Os Guinness, *Fit Bodies and Fat Minds: Why Evangelicals Don't Think* (London: Hodder & Stoughton, 1995), p. 51.

40. Jim Leffel, "Our New Challenge: Postmodernism," in McCallum, *The Death of Truth*, p. 31.

41. Gene E. Veith, *Guide to Contemporary Culture* (Leicester: Crossway Books, 1994), p. 19.

42. Carson, *The Gagging of God: Christianity Confronts Pluralism*, p. 35.

43. John Stott, *Your Mind Matters* (Downers Grove, IL: InterVarsity Press, 1972), p. 14.

44. Curtis Chang, *Engaging Unbelief* (Leicester: IVP Apollos, 2000), p. 31.

45. Stott, *Your Mind Matters*, p. 20.

46. Wim Rietkerk, *If Only I Could Believe!* (Carlisle, UK: Paternoster, 1997), p. xiii.

47. Lecture by Francis Schaeffer, "Basic Problem: Truth versus Contentless Experience," delivered at Swiss L'Abri in January 1964, Farel House tape no. 43.4.

48. Francis A. Schaeffer, *The New Super-Spirituality* (London: Hodder & Stoughton, 1973), p. 16.

49. David Wells, *God in the Wasteland* (Leicester: IVP, 1994), p. 40.

50. Lecture by Francis Schaeffer, "Apologetics," delivered at Swiss L'Abri, December 1963, Farel House tape no. Y483.

51. Francis A. Schaeffer, *The God Who Is There* (Leicester: IVP, 1968, 1990), p. 135.

52. Ibid., p. 144.

53. Lecture, "Apologetics."

54. Schaeffer, *The God Who Is There*, p. 138.

55. Ibid., p. 145.

56. Ibid., p. 142.

57. Burson and Walls, *C. S. Lewis and Francis Schaeffer: Lessons for a New Century from the Most Influential Apologists of Our Time*, p. 256.

58. Ibid., p. 255.

59. Ibid., p. 253.

60. Lecture, "Truth versus Contentless Experience."

61. Grenz, *A Primer on Postmodernism*, p. 165.

62. Millard J. Erickson, *Postmodernizing the Faith* (Grand Rapids, MI: Baker Books, 1998), p. 88.

63. Grenz, *A Primer on Postmodernism*, p. 161.

64. Ibid., p. 170.

65. Clark Pinnock, *Tracking the Maze: Finding Our Way Through Modern Theology from an Evangelical Perspective* (San Francisco: Harper & Row, 1990), pp. 182-183.

66. Grenz, *A Primer on Postmodernism*, p. 163.

67. Philip Kenneson, "There's No Such Thing as Objective Truth, and It's a Good Thing Too," in Timothy Phillips and Dennis Okholm, eds., *Christian Apologetics in the Postmodern World* (Downers Grove, IL: InterVarsity Press, 1995), p. 159.

68. Schaeffer, *The God Who Is There*, p. 121.
69. Francis A. Schaeffer, *He Is There and He Is Not Silent* (Leicester: IVP, 1972, 1990), p. 289.
70. Ibid., pp. 328, 334-335.
71. Lecture, "Truth versus Contentless Experience."
72. Schaeffer, *The God Who Is There*, p. 138.
73. David K. Clark, *Dialogical Apologetics: A Person-Centered Approach to Christian Defense* (Grand Rapids, MI: Baker Books, 1993), p. 124.
74. Jerram Barrs, *The Heart of Evangelism* (Leicester: IVP, 2001), p. 182.
75. Dick Keyes, *Beyond Identity* (Carlisle, UK: Paternoster, 1998) and Wim Rietkerk, *If Only I Could Believe!*
76. M. Walford-Dellu, "You Can Have a Family with Us," in Dennis, *Francis Schaeffer: Portraits of the Man and His Work*, p. 132.
77. For example, see Graham Cray, *Postmodern Culture and Youth Discipleship* (Cambridge: Grove Books, 1998); John Drane, *Cultural Change and Biblical Faith* (Carlisle, UK: Paternoster, 2000); Stuart Murray, *Church Planting: Laying Foundations* (Carlisle, UK: Paternoster, 1998); Brian McLaren, *A New Kind of Christian: A Tale of Two Friends on a Spiritual Journey* (San Francisco: Jossey-Bass, 2001); and Mike Yaconelli, ed., *Stories of Emergence: Moving from Absolutes to Authentic* (Grand Rapids, MI: Zondervan, 2003).
78. Murray, *Church Planting: Laying Foundations*, p. 187.
79. Drane, *Cultural Change and Biblical Faith*, p. 179.
80. Murray, *Church Planting: Laying Foundations*, p. 165.
81. Schaeffer, *The God Who Is There*, pp. 155-156.
82. Ibid., p. 156.
83. D. A. Carson, *Becoming Conversant with the Emerging Church* (Grand Rapids, MI: Zondervan, 2005), p. 187.
84. Lecture, "Truth versus Contentless Experience."
85. See in particular Acts 17–18.
86. Interview with John Stott in London on November 12, 1999.
87. Ibid.
88. Lecture, "Truth versus Contentless Experience."
89. Lecture, "Apologetics."
90. Schaeffer, *The God Who Is There*, p. 145.
91. For example, Brian McLaren, one of the leading writers in the emerging church movement, has a character in one of his books refer to substitu-

tionary atonement as sounding like "divine child abuse." Brian McLaren, *The Story We Find Ourselves In* (San Francisco: Jossey-Bass, 2003), p. 102.

92. John Drane, *The McDonaldization of the Church: Consumer Culture and the Church's Future* (Macon, GA: Smyth & Helwys, 2001), p. 185.

93. Stott interview.

94. Burson and Walls, *C. S. Lewis and Francis Schaeffer: Lessons for a New Century from the Most Influential Apologists of Our Time*, p. 270.

95. Francis A. Schaeffer, *Two Contents: Two Realities* (London: Hodder & Stoughton, 1974), p. 33.

96. Ibid., p. 34.

97. Ibid., pp. 30-32.

98. Schaeffer, *The Church Before the Watching World*, p. 62.

99. Schaeffer, *Two Contents: Two Realities*, p. 34.

100. Schaeffer, *The Church at the End of the Twentieth Century*, p. 90.

101. Schaeffer, *The Church Before the Watching World*, p. 63.

102. Schaeffer, *The Church at the End of the Twentieth Century*, pp. 168-170.

103. Ibid., p. 131.

104. Ibid., p. 134.

105. Ibid., p. 129.

106. Ibid., p. 131.

107. Edith Schaeffer, *The Tapestry*, p. 356.

108. Francis A. Schaeffer, *True Spirituality* (Wheaton, IL: Tyndale, 1971), p. 61.

109. Ibid., pp. 41-44.

110. Ibid., pp. 69-70.

111. Dennis, *Letters of Francis Schaeffer*, letter dated December 20, 1960, p. 82.

112. Schaeffer, *True Spirituality*, p. 70.

113. Burson and Walls, *C. S. Lewis and Francis Schaeffer: Lessons for a New Century from the Most Influential Apologists of Our Time*, p. 56.

114. Ibid., pp. 263-264.

115. Schaeffer, *True Spirituality*, p. 5.

116. Edith Schaeffer, *The Tapestry*, p. 357.

117. Schaeffer, *True Spirituality*, p. 74.

118. Ibid., pp. 76-77.

119. Dennis, *Letters of Francis Schaeffer*, letter dated November 12, 1954, p. 48.

120. Schaeffer, *True Spirituality*, p. 15.

121. See Revelation 2:1-7.

122. Schaeffer, *True Spirituality*, p. 158.

123. Dennis, *Letters of Francis Schaeffer*, letter dated November 12, 1954, p. 49.

124. Edith Schaeffer, *The Tapestry*, p. 209.

125. Ibid., pp. 189-190.

126. Sermon by Francis Schaeffer on "Prayer," given in the L'Abri Chapel at Huémoz on the first Sunday following its dedication in 1964. Farel House tape no. 24.2.

127. Ibid.

128. Edith Schaeffer, *L'Abri*, p. v.

129. Hurvey Woodson, interviewed on "L'Abri: Truth and Love," Part II of "The Story of Francis and Edith Schaeffer," produced by RBC Ministries for *Day of Discovery*, USA, 2003.

130. Francis A. Schaeffer, *No Little People*, in *The Complete Works of Francis A. Schaeffer*, Vol. 3 (Wheaton, IL: Crossway Books, 1982), p. 9.

131. Ibid., p. 12.

132. Priscilla Sandri, interviewed on "L'Abri: Truth and Love," Part II of "The Story of Francis and Edith Schaeffer."

133. Os Guinness, interviewed on "The Watching World," Part III of "The Story of Francis and Edith Schaeffer," produced by RBC Ministries for *Day of Discovery*, USA, 2003.

134. Schaeffer, *No Little People*, p. 14.